ECDL® 5.0

European Computer Driving Licence

Module 4 - Spreadsheets

Using Microsoft® Excel 2010

Release ECDL275v1

Published by:

CiA Training Ltd
Business & Innovation Centre
Sunderland Enterprise Park
Sunderland
SR5 2TA
United Kingdom

Tel: +44 (0) 191 549 5002
Fax: +44 (0) 191 549 9005

E-mail: info@ciatraining.co.uk
Web: www.ciatraining.co.uk

ISBN: 978-1-86005-854-7

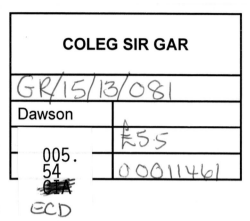

COLEG SIR GAR

GR/15/13/081

Dawson

005.54

£5·5

00011461

ECD

Important Note

This guide was written for *Microsoft Office 2010* running on *Windows 7*. If using earlier versions of *Windows* some dialog boxes may look and function slightly differently to that described.

A screen resolution of *1024x768* is assumed. Working at a different resolution (or with an application window which is not maximised) may change the look of the dynamic *Office 2010 Ribbon*, which changes to fit the space available.

For example, the **Editing Group** on a full *Ribbon* will contain several buttons, but if space is restricted it may be replaced by an **Editing Button** (which, when clicked, will display the full **Editing Group**).

First published 2010

Copyright © 2010 CiA Training Ltd

All rights reserved. No part of this publication may be reproduced, stored in a retrieval system, or transmitted in any form or by any means (electronic, mechanical, photocopying, recording or otherwise) without the prior written permission of CiA Training Limited.

Microsoft is a registered trademark and Windows is a trademark of the Microsoft Corporation. Screen images reproduced by permission of the Microsoft Corporation. All other trademarks in this book are acknowledged as the property of their respective owners.

Downloading the Data Files

The data files associated with these exercises must be downloaded from our website. Go to *www.ciatraining.co.uk/data* and follow the on screen instructions to download the appropriate data files.

By default, the data files will be installed to **CIA DATA FILES \ ECDL \ 4 Spreadsheets** in your **Documents** library\folder (or **My Documents** in *Windows XP*).

If you prefer, the data can be supplied on CD at an additional cost. Contact the Sales team at *info@ciatraining.co.uk*.

Aims

To provide the student with an understanding of fundamental spreadsheet concepts, practical experience in spreadsheet design and implementation of the basic functions involved within spreadsheets.

Objectives

After completing the guide the user will be able to:

- Work with spreadsheets and save them in different file formats

- Choose built in options, such as the Help function, within the application to enhance productivity

- Enter data into cells and use good practice in creating lists; select, sort, copy, move and delete data

- Edit rows and columns in a worksheet; copy, move, delete and appropriately rename worksheets

- Create mathematical and logical formulas using standard spreadsheet functions; use good practice in formula creation and be able to recognise error values in formulas

- Format numbers and text content in a spreadsheet

- Choose, create and format charts to communicate information meaningfully

- Adjust spreadsheet page settings and check and correct spreadsheet content before finally printing spreadsheets.

Assessment of Knowledge

At the end of this guide is a section called the **Record of Achievement Matrix**. Before the guide is started it is recommended that the user complete the matrix to measure the level of current knowledge.

Tick boxes are provided for each feature. **1** is for no knowledge, **2** some knowledge and **3** is for competent.

After working through a section, complete the **Record of Achievement** matrix for that section and only when competent in all areas move on to the next section.

Contents

Section 1
Getting Started

By the end of this Section you should be able to:

Understand Spreadsheet Principles

Start a Spreadsheet Program

Recognise the Spreadsheet Screen Layout

Use the Ribbon and Quick Access Toolbar

Use Help

Change Preferences

Close a Spreadsheet Program

To gain an understanding of the above features, work through the **Driving Lessons** in this **Section**.

For each **Driving Lesson**, read the **Park and Read** instructions, without touching the keyboard, then work through the numbered steps of the **Manoeuvres** on the computer. Complete the **Revision Exercise(s)** at the end of the section to test your knowledge.

Driving Lesson 1 - Starting Excel

🅿 Park and Read

A spreadsheet package is a computer program created specifically to help in the processing of tabular information, usually numbers. The spreadsheet stores information in rows (across the screen) and columns (down the screen), forming a worksheet (the *Excel* term for a spreadsheet).

Spreadsheets are most commonly used to manipulate figures. They can be used for accounting, cash flows, budgeting, forecasts, etc. Any job that involves the use of numbers can be done on a spreadsheet.

The biggest advantage that a spreadsheet has over other methods of manipulating data is its ability to constantly update figures without the user having to do any calculations. Once a spreadsheet is set up, its calculations will always be correct and any changes in data are automatically updated.

Spreadsheets can also take raw data and present it in an attractive way, with formatted tables and charts.

Manoeuvres

1. There are numerous ways to start *Excel* depending on how the computer has been set up. The following method is recommended for beginners. Starting the computer will automatically show the *Windows* **Desktop**.

    Click once on the **Start** button 🪟 (situated at the bottom left of the screen, on the **Taskbar**), to show the list of start options available. All *Windows* applications can be started from here.

2. Move the mouse pointer to **All Programs**.

3. Click the **Microsoft Office** folder to display its contents.

4. Click ▣ Microsoft Excel 2010 .

5. The spreadsheet program *Excel 2010* starts.

Driving Lesson 2 - The Excel Screen

▣ Park and Read

On starting, *Excel* displays a blank workbook, as below, named **Book1** as shown in the **Title Bar**. A **workbook** is a file that can contain many **worksheets** but has 3 by default.

↱ Manoeuvres

1. The *Excel* screen will be similar to the diagram below. Check the captions and identify the parts on the screen. **Sheet1** is displayed.

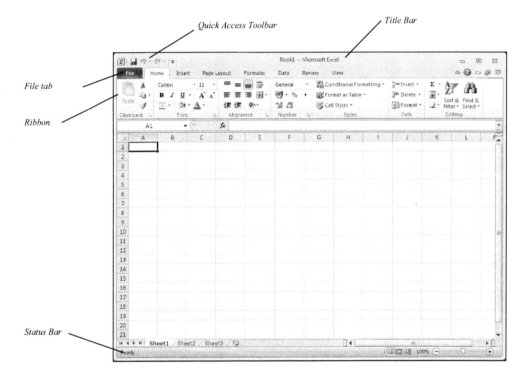

2. The **Title Bar** is the top line of the *Excel* screen. It shows the application and the name of the workbook that is on the screen. Identify the **Title Bar**.

3. The name of the current workbook is **Book1** or similar. Check this in the **Title Bar**.

continued over

Driving Lesson 2 - Continued

4.   At the top left of the screen the first tab on the **Ribbon** is the **File** tab, . This displays a list of basic program functions such as; **Open, Save, Print** and **Close**.

5.   Immediately above this button is the **Quick Access Toolbar**.

6.   By default this contains three buttons, **Save**, **Undo** and **Redo**. More buttons can be added to this toolbar.

7.   Under this toolbar is an area called the **Ribbon**. This consists of a range of tabs, containing buttons within groups. All commands are accessed using the ribbon.

8.   The buttons are used to select an action or basic feature. Move the cursor over any button but do not click. Read the **ToolTip**, which gives the name of that button, with a small description, e.g. **Italic** in the **Font** group.

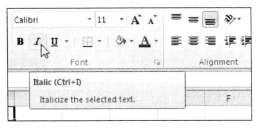

9.   The **Status Bar** runs along the bottom of the window. This displays messages as tasks are performed. Check that the current message, at the left, states **Ready**.

10. The right side of the **Status Bar** contains **Views** buttons and a **Zoom** slider.

11. Along the bottom of the screen is the **Taskbar**, this contains the **Start** button, open application buttons and others, including **Time**.

Driving Lesson 3 - The Ribbon

Park and Read

Excel 2010 has a **Ribbon** which is displayed at the top of the application window, this replaces the menus and toolbars from earlier versions. The **Ribbon** contains buttons and drop down lists to control the operation of *Excel*. The **Ribbon** is divided into a series of **Tabs**, each one of which has a set of controls specific to a certain function or process. On each tab, the controls are further divided into separate **Groups** of connected functions.

Some tabs can be selected manually, some only appear when certain operations are active, for example only when a **Chart** is active, will three **Chart Tools** tabs be displayed on the **Ribbon**.

Manoeuvres

1. On the **Ribbon**, the **Home** tab should be selected. Other basic tabs, are available.

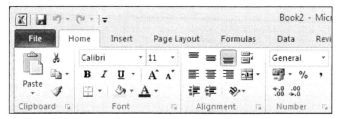

*Part of the **Ribbon** displaying the **Home** tab*

> Any buttons displayed in pale grey are called ghosted and are not available to be selected at present.

2. Notice how the buttons on the **Ribbon** are divided into **Groups** (**Clipboard**, **Font**, **Alignment**, etc.).

> The display of buttons on the Ribbon is dynamic. That is it will change according to how much space there is available. If the window is not maximised or the screen resolution is anything other than 1024 by 768, the Ribbon will not always appear as shown in this guide.

3. Leave the cursor over any of the buttons. A **ToolTip** appears which give more information and an alternative key press for the function if available.

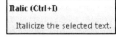

4. Some buttons produce immediate effects, like the **Bold**, **Italic** and **Underline** buttons in the **Font** group.

continued over

Driving Lesson 3 - Continued

5. Buttons with a drop down arrow lead to further options. Click the **Find & Select** button, which is found in the **Editing** group. A list of further options is displayed.

6. Some options will display a dialog box which needs data to be entered. Click the first option **Find**, the **Find and Replace** dialog box is displayed. Click the **Close** button in the dialog box to remove it.

7. Some groups have a dialog box launcher to the right of the group name, e.g. the **Font** group, ⌐‾‾‾Font‾‾‾⌐.

8. Click the **Font** dialog box launcher to display the **Format Cells** dialog box.

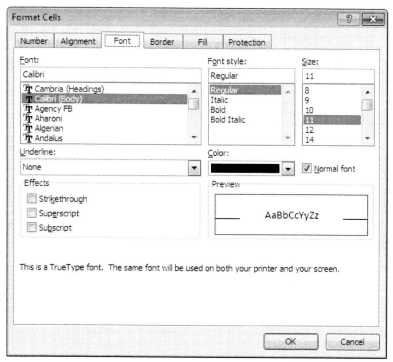

9. This is a tabbed dialog box, similar to those used in previous versions of *Excel*. Click **Cancel** to close the **Format Cells** dialog box.

10. Display the other basic tabs, one at a time, **Insert**, **Page Layout**, **Formulas**, **Data**, **Review** and **View** to see which other commands are available.

> 🛈 *There may be a **Developer** tab displayed, used for controlling macros. This tab is not displayed by default.*

11. Select the **Home** tab again.

Driving Lesson 4 - Quick Access Toolbar

▣ Park and Read

All the available commands are accessed via the **Ribbon**. Above the **Ribbon** is the **Quick Access Toolbar** which contains a few popular command buttons. By default this toolbar has three buttons, **Save**, **Undo** and **Redo**. This toolbar can be customised by adding further buttons.

⟰ Manoeuvres

1. Locate the **Quick Access Toolbar**.

2. Point at each button and read its **ToolTip**. There have been no actions performed yet, so the last two buttons are ghosted, but they still have ToolTips.

3. The third button is the **Redo** button. This button is used after **Undo** has been used, to reverse the undo.

4. To the right of the **Redo** button is the **Customize Quick Access Toolbar** button, ⬓. Click the button to display the menu.

5. To add commands not shown, either check an option or use **More Commands**. This displays **Excel Options,** which is covered later in the **Preferences** exercise.

6. Minimize the **Ribbon** by clicking the **Minimize the Ribbon** button, ⌃, which is located in the top right of the screen, to the left of the **Help** button.

7. The **Ribbon** is hidden with only the **Ribbon** tabs displayed. The ribbon is accessed by clicking the tabs. Click **Home**, the complete **Home** tab is displayed, from which a selection can be made.

8. Click on a cell in the worksheet window. The **Home** tab contents are hidden again.

9. To restore the **Ribbon**, click the **Expand the Ribbon** button, ♡. The **Ribbon** is displayed normally again.

ℹ *The **Ribbon** can also be minimized by right clicking on it and selecting the **Minimize the Ribbon** option. To restore the **Ribbon** right click on any tab and uncheck **Minimize the Ribbon**.*

Driving Lesson 5 - The Worksheet Window

▣ Park and Read

Spreadsheets help in the processing of numbers. They store information arranged in **rows** (across the screen) and **columns** (down the screen). A **cell** is the intersection of a row and column. It is good practice for each filled cell to contain only a single element of data.

All the cells form a **worksheet** (the *Excel* term for a spreadsheet). Several **worksheets** are bound together and called a **workbook**.

↱ Manoeuvres

1. Each cell is identified by the column letter and row number, which form the intersection, e.g. the cell formed where column **D** and row **8** meet is known as cell **D8**. Move the mouse pointer to cell **B3** and click. The **Current** or **Active** cell is now **B3**. It has a dark border.

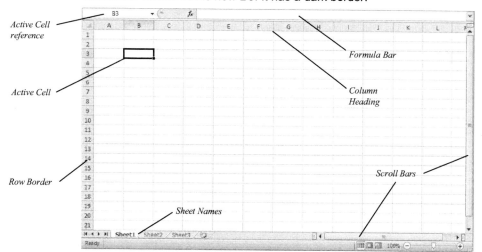

2. Look for the **Active Cell Reference**, which is shown in the **Name Box** at the left of the **Formula Bar**. It displays **B3**.

3. Click in cell **C6**. The **Active Cell Reference** now shows **C6**. These letters and numbers are shown highlighted in the **Row** and **Column Headings** on the worksheet. **C6** is now the **Current** or **Active cell**.

4. The active cell can be moved using various key presses. Press the right cursor key →. The active cell moves right into cell **D6**.

5. Press the down cursor ↓ to move into cell **D7**. Press the left cursor ← to move into **C7**.

6. Press the up cursor ↑. The active cell should now be **C6** again.

Driving Lesson 6 - Moving Around

⊞ Park and Read

A worksheet is very large. The arrow keys are used for moving small distances. Other keys are used to move bigger distances.

↷ Manoeuvres

1. Use the right cursor key → repeatedly to move to the column after **Z**. The alphabet is used again with **A** in front, i.e. **AA AB ...**, then **BA, BB ...**, etc.

2. The **<End>** key followed by an arrow key moves to the edge of the worksheet when empty. To move to the last column press **<End>** then the right arrow key →. The last column is **XFD** (column 16384).

3. Press the **<Home>** key, this always returns the active cell to column **A** on the same row.

4. Click on cell **D3**. Press **<End>** followed by the → key to move to **XFD3**.

5. Press the **<Home>** key to return to cell **A3**.

6. Press **<End>** then the **Down** cursor key ↓. The active cell moves down to the last row, **1048576**.

7. Press **<Ctrl Home>** (hold down the **Control** key and press the **Home** key) to move back to cell **A1**. The key press **<Ctrl Home>** always moves the active cell back to **A1**.

8. Click on a cell in the centre of the screen and press **<Ctrl Home>** to move to **A1**.

There are other key presses and mouse actions that also move the active cell around a worksheet. These are covered later when a workbook is opened that has cell contents added.

Driving Lesson 7 - Help

🅿 Park and Read

Excel has a comprehensive **Help** facility. This means that full advantage can be taken of the features incorporated in the program. Using **Help** can usually solve the majority of problems encountered.

Help topics are available either from **Office.com** via the internet, or from the content installed on your computer (offline). The method of using **Help** is the same in either case but the content may vary slightly.

☞ Manoeuvres

1. Click the **Help** button, 🔘 in the upper right corner of the *Excel* window to display the **Excel Help** window.

ℹ️ *Pressing the <F1> key will display the same **Help** window. The window can be moved, resized or maximised if required.*

2. If the **Table of Contents** panel is not displayed on the left, as shown below, click the **Show Table of Contents** button, ✅, on the **Help** toolbar.

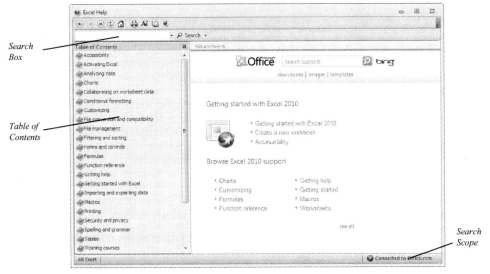

3. The **Search Scope** button at the bottom of the window indicates whether you are connected to **Office.com** or not (offline). Click on the button to see the available options, and make sure **Show content from Office.com** is selected.

continued over

Driving Lesson 7 - Continued

i *The content and appearance of the information provided by the online* **Help** *system will possibly change over time and may not be exactly as shown here.*

4. **Help** can be used in two ways. You can either browse through the listed topics or type keywords into the **Search** box.

5. A list of categories is shown on the opening screen in the main display area. Click on any one that interests you to display a list of relevant hyperlinked topics.

6. Scan the topics shown and click any that are of interest.

i *The same information can be found using by navigating the* **Table of Contents***.*

7. To move back to a previous screen, click the **Back** button, ⬅, on the dialog box toolbar. You can then follow another link.

i *Help topics can be printed for reference by clicking the* **Print** *button,* 🖨.

8. Click the **Home** button, 🏠, on the dialog box toolbar to return directly to the starting help screen.

9. Another way to find help is to search by keyword. Type **shortcuts** into the **Search** box and click the **Search** button, 🔍 Search ▾.

Search results for: **shortcuts**

Keyboard **shortcuts** for Clip Organizer
    Article | Toolbar shortcuts To do this Press Display the Collection List task pane ALT+C...

Keyboard **shortcuts** for SmartArt graphics
    Article | The keyboard shortcuts described in this Help topic refer to the U.S. keyboard l...

Accessibility Features in Microsoft Office 2010
    Article | Microsoft Office 2010 continues the dedication to both making Microsoft Offic...

Keyboard **shortcuts** in Excel 2010
    Article | This article describes what Key Tips are and how you can use them to access th...

---

i *There may be many topics found for your search and it will be necessary for you to use your own judgement and select the most appropriate one.*

10. Click the **Home** button, 🏠, to return to the starting screen.

i *The* **Table of Contents** *can be hidden by clicking the* **Hide Table of Contents** *button,* 📖*, on the* **Help** *toolbar.*

11. Close the **Help** window by clicking its **Close** button, ⊠.

Driving Lesson 8 - Preferences

▣ Park and Read

Basic **Excel Options** (preferences) can be changed, for example, the user name, which is added to certain templates. By default workbooks are opened from, and saved to, the **Documents** library. These locations can also be changed.

↱ Manoeuvres

1. Click the **File** tab, **File** and then select **Options**. This dialog box sets and controls user preferences.

2. Display each option in turn and scroll down to view the available preferences. Do not make any changes.

3. Select the **General** option.

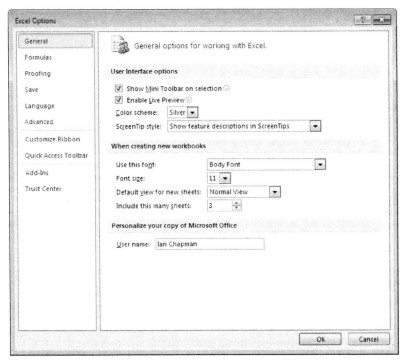

4. To change the user details enter your own name in **User name**.

5. Select the **Save** option, from the list at the left.

continued over

Driving Lesson 8 - Continued

6.   Note that the **Default file location** is the **Documents** folder.

7.   This location can be changed to any folder on your computer, e.g. the working folder for this module is:

   …..Documents\CIA DATA FILES\ECDL\4 Spreadsheets

   and this could be entered in the **Default file location** box. Setting the **Default file location** is a useful feature and will save time when opening and saving files. However, the location above could only be used temporarily while completing this guide. The setting would then need changing again. Leave the default location as **Documents**.

8.   Click **OK**.

9.   Click the **File** tab, select the **Info** option then click the **Properties** drop down arrow and select **Show Document Panel**. The **Document Properties** panel is now displayed underneath the ribbon.

10.   Each workbook has a **Document Properties** attached. The author name is taken from **User name** in **Options**. The **Author** name shown is still the previous one. Your name will be displayed as the **Author** for every new workbook started from now.

11.   The information is saved with the workbook. The location changes to the full path after saving. Close the **Document Properties** by clicking its close button (in the top right of the panel).

Driving Lesson 9 - Closing Excel

▣ Park and Read

If any workbooks are still open when *Excel* is closed, a warning will be displayed with an option to save the changes.

⚐ Manoeuvres

1.   Click the **File** tab, **File** to display the menu.

2.   Click **Info** on the left if this is not already selected and look at the options available.

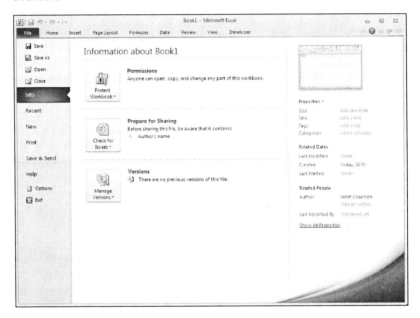

3.   Click **Exit** and *Excel* closes, however, if an open workbook needs saving because of changes then a save prompt is displayed. Select **Don't Save** if there is a prompt to save.

ℹ️ *Excel can also be closed by clicking the **Close** button,* ⊠ *in the top right corner of the screen or by pressing <**Alt F4**>.*

Driving Lesson 10 - Revision

This Driving Lesson covers the features introduced in this section. Try not to refer to the preceding Driving Lessons while completing it.

1. Start *Excel* using the **Start** button.

2. How is the **Active Cell** displayed?

3. How many worksheets are in a workbook by default?

4. Use the mouse pointer to find **ToolTips** for the following buttons, located on the **Home** tab:

    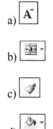

5. How many groups are displayed on the **Data** tab of the **Ribbon**?

6. The **Formulas** tab has the following groups: **Function Library**, **Calculation**, **Formula Auditing** and which other?

7. Close down *Excel* using the **File** tab. What is the option called that actually closes the application down?

ⓘ *Answers are shown in the **Answers** section at the end of this guide.*

If you experienced any difficulty completing this Revision refer back to the Driving Lessons in this section. Then redo the Revision.

Driving Lesson 11 - Revision

This Driving Lesson covers the features introduced in this section. Try not to refer to the preceding Driving Lessons while completing it.

1. Start *Excel*.

2. What function does the key combination<**Alt F4**> perform?

3. How many buttons are on the **Quick Access Toolbar**, by default and what are they called?

4. With a key press move to the last column on the worksheet, **XFD**. What did you press?

5. Move down to the last row on the worksheet, what is the row number?

6. Return to cell **A1** with a key press. What did you press?

7. There are two ways to start **Help**, one way is to use the **Microsoft Office Excel Help** button. What is the other?

8. Start **Excel Help**.

9. Search for **preview**. Find a topic on previewing a file.

10. Return to the original screen. What button did you use?

11. Using the **Topics** list find the same information. What is it stored under?

12. Close **Help**.

13. Leave *Excel* open for the next section.

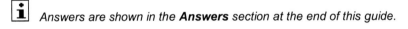 *Answers are shown in the **Answers** section at the end of this guide.*

If you experienced any difficulty completing this Revision refer back to the Driving Lessons in this section. Then redo the Revision.

Once you are confident with the features, complete the Record of Achievement Matrix referring to the section at the end of the guide. Only when competent move on to the next Section.

Section 2
Open and Close
Workbooks

By the end of this Section you should be able to:

Open a Workbook

Open Multiple Workbooks

Use Scroll Bars

Close a Workbook

To gain an understanding of the above features, work through the **Driving Lessons** in this **Section**.

For each **Driving Lesson**, read the **Park and Read** instructions, without touching the keyboard, then work through the numbered steps of the **Manoeuvres** on the computer. Complete the **Revision Exercise(s)** at the end of the section to test your knowledge.

Driving Lesson 12 - Opening a Workbook

▣ Park and Read

Workbooks saved to disk can be opened to use again.

↱ Manoeuvres

1. To open an existing workbook, click the **File** tab, then click **Open** from the list. This will display the **Open** dialog box. **Documents** is the default location.

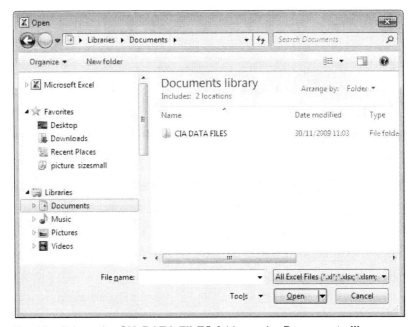

2. Double click on the **CIA DATA FILES** folder under **Documents library**.

3. Double click the **ECDL**.

4. Double click on **4 Spreadsheets** to display the data files used with this module.

5. Change the view to **List** if necessary, using the **Views** button drop down,

continued over

Driving Lesson 12 - Continued

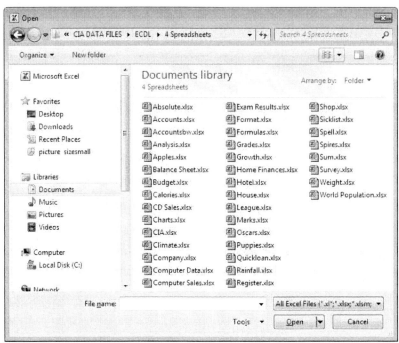

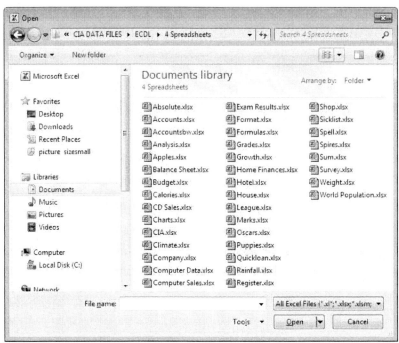 This guide assumes that the folder being used for the storage of files is **CIA DATA FILES\ECDL\4 Spreadsheets** *on the hard drive. If this is not the case, then select the appropriate drive/disk and folder.*

6. The *Excel* files will be displayed. *Excel* can also display files of other types if necessary by selecting from **Files of type** box, to the right of the **File name** box.

7. In the list of files, click on **Hotel**, the workbook to be opened. Click the **Open** button.

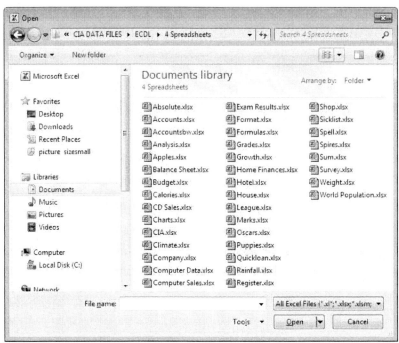 *The file can also be opened by double clicking on its name in the list.*

 Office 2010 *can find files by starting to type the file name in the box. Select from the list and then click open. This action saves time when faced with a folder with a large number of files, where scrolling would be needed.*

Driving Lesson 13 - Closing a Workbook

☐ Park and Read

If a workbook is to no longer to be used at this time, it needs to be closed.

☞ Manoeuvres

1. The workbook **Hotel** should still be on the screen from the previous Driving Lesson. If not, then open it.

2. Click the **File** tab and then **Close** to close the workbook. If changes had been made to the workbook, the following dialog box would be displayed to prevent the accidental loss of the changes.

3. In this instance, no changes have been made to the workbook, so it should close without displaying the dialog box (if the dialog box does appear, click on **Don't Save,** which will close the file <u>without</u> saving).

> ℹ️ *If closing a workbook created in an earlier version of Excel, a slightly different dialog box will be shown.*

> ℹ️ *The **Close Window** button can be used to close the workbook. Be careful not to close Excel by clicking the **Close** button. The key press <**Ctrl W**> can also be used to close the active window.*

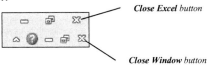

Close Excel *button*

Close Window *button*

4. There should be no **Workbooks** open. If there are, click the **File** tab and select **Close** until the screen is different: the centre part is blank and most of the buttons are ghosted.

> ℹ️ *If a blank workbook is still displayed, close it, click the **File** tab and select **Close**.*

Driving Lesson 14 - Using Scroll Bars

🅿 Park and Read

Small movements between adjacent cells are usually achieved using the cursor keys. However, when moving to a different area of the worksheet, the mouse and **Scroll Bars** are used.

Manoeuvres

1. Open the workbook **Oscars** and click on cell **C3** to make it the **Active Cell**.

2. The screen has a horizontal and vertical scroll bar, which can be used to scroll around the worksheet.

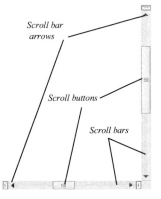

Scroll bar arrows

Scroll buttons

Scroll bars

3. Click the down arrow of the vertical scroll bar to view more of the worksheet, by one row. Continue to do this until row **6** is at the top of the screen. If you go too far this can be reversed by clicking on the up arrow.

4. Click the right arrow of the horizontal scroll bar to view one more column of the worksheet. Continue to do this until column **D** is at the left of the screen.

5. Notice that the **Active Cell Reference** field still reads **C3**. Even though it is not currently on the screen, **C3** is still the **Active Cell**.

6. To move a whole screen view down, click once on the vertical scroll bar between the scroll button and the bottom arrow.

7. To move a whole screen view to the right, click once on the horizontal scroll bar between the scroll button and the right arrow.

8. Now click the vertical scroll button and drag it up slowly a small amount. The work area scrolls continuously up until the mouse button is released.

9. Drag the horizontal scroll button to the left. The work area scrolls horizontally.

10. Now use the scroll buttons to view cell **A1**, then click on cell **B3** to make it the active cell.

11. Use the scroll buttons to scroll to the right and down as far as possible. Press **<Enter>**, this moves the active cell down to **B4**. The worksheet view will reset so that the new active cell, **B4** is in the top left corner.

12. Close the workbook <u>without</u> saving.

Driving Lesson 15 - Opening Multiple Workbooks

▣ Park and Read

More than one workbook can be open at the same time.

↱ Manoeuvres

1. Open the workbook **Spires**.

2. Without closing the **Spires** workbook, open the workbook **Grades**.

3. Both of these workbooks are now open. Click on the **Excel** button in the **Taskbar**. By default, each open workbook is listed above the button.

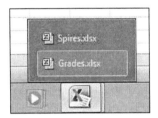

ℹ️ *Alternative views are possible, with each workbook shown as a separate button. There may also be many other buttons on the **Taskbar** depending on which other applications are running.*

4. Notice how the option representing the workbook **Grades** being viewed is highlighted, showing that it is active.

5. Click **Spires** in the list to view that workbook. This workbook is now active.

6. Open the workbook **Budget**. The **Excel** button now when clicked shows three workbooks in the list.

7. Which workbook after clicking the **Excel** button on the **Taskbar** is highlighted?

ℹ️ *The key press <Alt Tab> can be used to switch from window to window.*

8. Display **Spires**.

9. Close all the open workbooks <u>without</u> saving.

ℹ️ *Answers are shown in the **Answers** section at the end of this guide.*

Driving Lesson 16 - Revision

This is Driving Lesson covers the features introduced in this section. Try not to refer to the preceding Driving Lessons while completing it.

1. Open the workbook **Hotel**.

2. Use the scroll bars to navigate to the edges of the blocks of occupied cells.

3. Make **A1** the active cell in the **Hotel** workbook.

4. Scroll down with the scroll button to display **Row 15** as the first row on the screen.

5. Leave the **Hotel** workbook open and open the workbook **Grades**.

6. Make **Hotel** the active workbook.

7. Close the workbook **Hotel** <u>without</u> saving.

8. Close the workbook **Grades** <u>without</u> saving.

If you experienced any difficulty completing this Revision refer back to the Driving Lessons in this section. Then redo the Revision.

Once you are confident with the features, complete the Record of Achievement Matrix referring to the section at the end of the guide. Only when competent move on to the next Section.

Section 3
Creating and Saving Workbooks

By the end of this Section you should be able to:

Start a New Workbook

Enter Text and Numbers

Save a New and Named Workbook

Save Workbooks in Different Formats

Save a Workbook as a Template

To gain an understanding of the above features, work through the **Driving Lessons** in this **Section**.

For each **Driving Lesson**, read the **Park and Read** instructions, without touching the keyboard, then work through the numbered steps of the **Manoeuvres** on the computer. Complete the **Revision Exercise(s)** at the end of the section to test your knowledge.

Driving Lesson 17 - Starting a New Workbook

▣ Park and Read

A blank workbook based on the default template must be started to begin creating a new spreadsheet.

↱ Manoeuvres

1. Start a new workbook by clicking the **File** tab and selecting **New**.

2. Examine the top of the list at the left. There are options to: start a new blank workbook, create one from an existing workbook and create a new workbook from an existing template.

3. The **Blank workbook** is the default option, click the **Create** button to start a new workbook.

4. Leave this blank workbook open for the next Driving Lesson.

Driving Lesson 18 - Entering Labels

🄿 Park and Read

Labels are normally used for describing the contents of the worksheet, as columns or row titles. When entering information into a cell, notice that the text appears in the **Formula Bar** as well as in the cell. A cell should really only ever contain one data item, e.g. a first name in one cell and a surname in an adjacent cell. This makes the data much easier to manipulate and sort. It's also good practice when creating a list of data to make sure it's easy to read. You can use a variety of layouts to do this: leave cells surrounding the list blank, leave a blank row before a row showing totals. Make sure you don't leave blank rows or columns in the main part of the list though.

⌒ Manoeuvres

1. With a blank workbook on screen, click on cell **A3** to select it.

2. Type the label **Fruit**. Notice **Enter** appears on the **Status Bar**, and that the **Enter** button appears in the **Formula Bar**. Press the <**Enter**> key to place the label into cell **A3**.

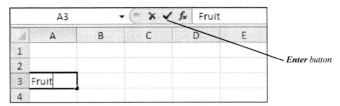

Enter button

[i] *The entry can also be completed by clicking on the Enter button.*

3. Move to cell **B3** and type **Apples**. Place **Apples** in **B3** by pressing the right cursor key →. This automatically enters the data into **B3** and moves the active cell to the right, ready for the next entry.

4. Pressing <**Enter**> moves the selection down, by default. Click the **File** tab and then click **Options**. Display the **Advanced** options and check that the **Direction** is **Down** under **After pressing Enter, move selection**.

	A	B	C	D	E
1					
2					
3	Fruit	Apples	Pears	Oranges	Total
4	Jan				
5	Feb				
6	Mar				
7	Total				
8					

Click **OK**. Complete the entries into the cells as opposite. If any mistakes are made, leave the errors.

5. Leave the workbook open for the next Driving Lesson.

Driving Lesson 19 - Entering Numbers

Park and Read

Numbers must begin with one of the following characters: **0 1 2 3 4 5 6 7 8 9 . + -** or a currency symbol.

Manoeuvres

1.   Use the workbook open from the previous Driving Lesson.

2.   Click on cell **B4** and type **36**, followed by **<Enter>**. The active cell is placed in cell **B5** ready for the next entry.

3.   Enter the rest of the information into the correct cells, using the cursor movement keys to complete each entry.

	A	B	C	D	E	F
1						
2						
3	Fruit	Apples	Pears	Oranges	Total	
4	Jan	36	38	26		
5	Feb	40	26	37		
6	Mar	53	20	41		
7	Total					
8						

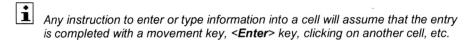

*Any instruction to enter or type information into a cell will assume that the entry is completed with a movement key, <**Enter**> key, clicking on another cell, etc.*

4.   Do **NOT** close the workbook as it is saved in a later Driving Lesson.

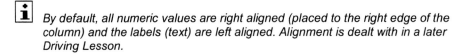

By default, all numeric values are right aligned (placed to the right edge of the column) and the labels (text) are left aligned. Alignment is dealt with in a later Driving Lesson.

Driving Lesson 20 - Saving a New Workbook

⊞ Park and Read

After creating a worksheet, it needs to be saved as a workbook so it can be used again. The **Save** process includes selecting the location to save to, giving the workbook a name and selecting the type of format to save it in.

⌐ Manoeuvres

1. With the worksheet open from the previous Driving Lesson, click the **Save** button, 🖫 on the **Quick Access Toolbar**, or click the **File** tab and select **Save As** or use the key press <**Ctrl S**> to display the **Save As** dialog box.

2. In the **File name** box overtype to change the default workbook name to **Fruit**. The files for this guide are stored in the **4 Spreadsheets** folder. (see Page 4 **Downloading the Data Files** for the exact location).

ℹ️ *After moving to the **4 Spreadsheets** folder earlier, Excel remains there until it is closed down or another location is selected. Excel, when restarted, will revert to the default folder, **Documents**.*

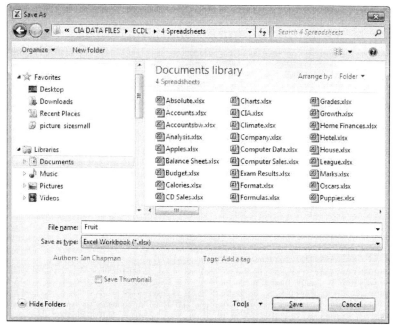

3. Click the **Save** button to save the file, then check the **Title Bar** for the file name.

4. Leave the workbook **Fruit** open.

Driving Lesson 21 - Saving a Named Workbook

▣ Park and Read

There are two commands used when saving a workbook.

Save	saves the file under the same name as previously used and overwrites an earlier version.
Save As	allows changes to be made to the initial save options creating a different version of the original, or to overwrite the original by confirming the replacement. This option can be used to create a backup of a file to a diskette (a floppy disk) or a memory stick.

⌒ Manoeuvres

1. The workbook **Fruit** should still be on screen from the last Driving Lesson. Select cell **A1** and enter your name, then complete the entry.

2. This workbook will now be saved as **Fruit2**. Click the **File** tab and then **Save As** to display the dialog box.

3. Type or edit the name in the **File name** box to **Fruit2** to save the file with the new name. Check that the current folder (in which to save the file) is correct in the folder box.

4. Click **Save**.

5. This workbook has not changed but it can still be saved to overwrite the first copy. Click the **File** tab and then **Save As**, leave the filename as **Fruit2**, click the **Save** button to begin saving.

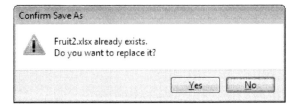

6. Click **Yes** to replace the existing file. The workbook is saved.

7. Close the workbook **Fruit2**.

8. *Excel* displays the most recently opened workbooks on the **File** menu, under **Recent**. Open the workbook **Fruit** by clicking the **File** tab and then clicking on **Fruit**. It should be exactly as saved earlier, i.e. without your name.

9. Close the workbook **Fruit**.

Driving Lesson 22 - Saving in Different Formats

▣ Park and Read

Workbooks can be saved in a variety of formats: Text, template, older versions of *Excel* and associated products.

⌐ Manoeuvres

1. Open the workbook **Grades**. This workbook cannot be opened in older versions of *Excel* or other spreadsheet programs without being saved in the correct format. To save the workbook in a different format. Click the **File** tab and **Save As**.

2. In the **File name** box enter **Test Format**, then click the drop down arrow of **Save as type** box.

3. Scan the list to display all the available formats that *Excel* can use. Choose the **Excel 97-2003 Workbook (*.xls)**, a set of previous *Excel* versions. Click **Save**.

Excel Workbook (*.xlsx)
Excel Macro-Enabled Workbook (*.xlsm)
Excel Binary Workbook (*.xlsb)
Excel 97-2003 Workbook (*.xls)
XML Data (*.xml)
Single File Web Page (*.mht;*.mhtml)
Web Page (*.htm;*.html)
Excel Template (*.xltx)
Excel Macro-Enabled Template (*.xltm)
Excel 97-2003 Template (*.xlt)
Text (Tab delimited) (*.txt)
Unicode Text (*.txt)
XML Spreadsheet 2003 (*.xml)
Microsoft Excel 5.0/95 Workbook (*.xls)
CSV (Comma delimited) (*.csv)
Formatted Text (Space delimited) (*.prn)
Text (Macintosh) (*.txt)
Text (MS-DOS) (*.txt)
CSV (Macintosh) (*.csv)
CSV (MS-DOS) (*.csv)
DIF (Data Interchange Format) (*.dif)
SYLK (Symbolic Link) (*.slk)
Excel Add-In (*.xlam)
Excel 97-2003 Add-In (*.xla)
PDF (*.pdf)
XPS Document (*.xps)
OpenDocument Spreadsheet (*.ods)

4. To save the file so that it can be opened in another application's format display **Save As** and from the **Save as type** box, select **CSV (Comma delimited) (*.csv)**. Change the file name to **Test2**. Click **Save**.

5. If a workbook contains features that are not supported in the chosen format, an error message is displayed about losing formatting. Click **Yes** to lose some formatting. The workbook is saved as **Test2.csv**. This file can be opened by other spreadsheet applications.

6. To save the workbook as a specific software file, display **Save As** and from the **Save as type** box, select **OpenDocument Spreadsheet (*.ods)** and change the file name to **Test3**. Click **Save**. Select **Yes** at the prompt. The workbook is saved as **Test3.ods**. This file can be opened in other applications that support it, e.g. *OpenOffice*.

7. To save the workbook as a text file, display **Save As** and from the **Save as type** box, select **Text (Tab delimited) (*.txt)** and change the file name to **Test4**. Click **Save**. Select **Yes** at the prompt. The workbook is saved as **Test4.txt**. This text file can be opened in *Notepad*, *WordPad* or *Word*.

8. Close the text file. Click **Don't Save** to the save the changes message.

Driving Lesson 23 - Saving as a Template

Park and Read

An *Excel* worksheet can be saved as a **Template**, so that it can be viewed as a starting point from which to create new worksheets.

Manoeuvres

1. Open the workbook **Grades**.

2. To save the workbook as a template, click the **File** tab and then **Save As**. In the **Save As** dialog box, change the **File name** to **Scores** and from **Save as type** select **Excel Template (*.xltx)**.

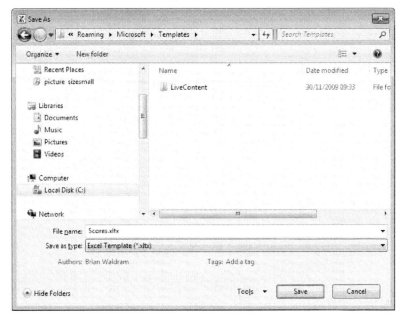

3. Click **Save**.

 *A **Template** is a base workbook that is stored with other templates. They have an .xltx extension and are shown with a ⬛, icon. To use a template select the **File** tab then **New** and then select **My templates**. Available templates will be displayed in the **New** dialog box in the **Personal Templates** tab.*

4. Close the workbook.

5. Select to open a file. Note that the **Templates** folder is still displayed. After saving a template you will need to navigate back to the data files folder. Navigate to the **4 Spreadsheets** folder, then click **Cancel**.

Driving Lesson 24 - Revision

This Driving Lesson covers the features introduced in this section. Try not to refer to the preceding Driving Lessons while completing it.

1.   Start with a new workbook.

2.   Create the following worksheet in the columns and rows indicated.

	A	B	C	D	E	F
1	Fred Bloggs					
2						
3	Number	Add	Subtract	Multiply	Divide	
4	First	6	7	5	12	
5	Second	3	4	3	4	
6	Result					
7						

3.   Save the workbook as **Maths** and close it.

4.   Start a new workbook.

5.   Create the following worksheet:

	A	B	C	D
1	Formatting Section			
2				
3	Exercise	Title		
4		39	General Formatting	
5		40	Format Cells	
6		41	Format Number	
7		42	Date and Time	
8		43	Alignment	
9		44	Wrap Text	
10		45	Merge Cells	
11		46	Text Orientation	
12		47	Borders	
13		48	Revision	
14				

6.   Save the workbook as **Formatting Section** and close it.

If you experienced any difficulty completing this Revision refer back to the Driving Lessons in this section. Then redo the Revision.

Driving Lesson 25 - Revision

This Driving Lesson covers the features introduced in this section. Try not to refer to the preceding Driving Lessons while completing it.

1.   Start with a new workbook.

2.   Create the following worksheet in the columns and rows indicated.

	A	B	C	D	E	F	G	H	I
1	Satellite Sales Figures								
2									
3		Mon	Tue	Wed	Thu	Fri	Sat	Sun	Total
4	Zara	0	3	5	3	2	4	5	
5	George	4	5	3	0	7	6	2	
6	Ishmael	3	2	0	6	4	5	3	
7	Liz	3	6	2	4	5	10	0	
8	Total								
9									

3.   Save the workbook as **Satellite**.

4.   Save the workbook as **Satellite97** in a worksheet format that can be opened in **Excel 97**.

5.   Close the workbook **Satellite97**.

6.   Open the workbook **Quickloan**.

7.   Save the worksheet as a **template**, as **Loan**.

8.   Close the workbook.

9.   Open the workbook **Calories**.

10.   Enter your name in cell **A3**.

11.   Test the calories counter, using your own details.

12.   Save the workbook as a **template**, named **Calorie Intake**.

13.   Close the workbook.

If you experienced any difficulty completing this Revision refer back to the Driving Lessons in this section. Then redo the Revision.

Once you are confident with the features, complete the Record of Achievement Matrix referring to the section at the end of the guide. Only when competent move on to the next Section.

Section 4
Formulas

By the end of this Section you should be able to:

Enter Basic Formulas

Use AutoSum

Check Formulas

Check Spelling

To gain an understanding of the above features, work through the **Driving Lessons** in this **Section**.

For each **Driving Lesson**, read the **Park and Read** instructions, without touching the keyboard, then work through the numbered steps of the **Manoeuvres** on the computer. Complete the **Revision Exercise(s)** at the end of the section to test your knowledge.

Driving Lesson 26 - Formulas

▣ Park and Read

A calculation in *Excel* is called a **Formula**.

All formulas begin with an equals = sign, followed by the calculation. The calculation consists of cell references or numbers separated by a mathematical symbol (+ add, - subtract, * multiply, / divide), e.g. **=A1+A2**.

Formulas are used to calculate answers from numbers that are entered on to a sheet. To create formulas properly you should enter the cell references of those cells used in the calculation, rather than just typing in the numbers. This means that if the numbers in these cells are changed later, the formulas will be recalculated and will still be correct.

↱ Manoeuvres

1. Start a new workbook, move the cell pointer to **B2** and type in **66**. Move to cell **B3** and type **34**.

2. Move to cell **B4** and enter the formula to add the contents of cells **B2** and **B3** by typing in **=B2+B3 <Enter>**. Click in cell **B4** and note the cell display of **100** and the formula in the **Formula Bar**.

3. In **B6** type in this formula, which divides B2 by B3: **=B2/B3**. The answer is **1.941176**.

4. Move to cell **A8** and enter the following numbers (use the right directional arrow to complete each entry) into these cells:

    A8 **35**, B8 **23**, C8 **56**, D8 **99**, E8 **55**.

5. Move to cell **F8** and type in this formula **=A8+B8+C8+D8+E8 <Enter>**. The answer should be **268**.

6. Move back to cell **F8** and enter an = sign to begin the formula. Select cell **A8**, it appears in the **Formula Bar**. Type in the **+** symbol, then select cell **B8** and continue entering the **+** symbol and selecting the other cells until the formula is complete. Press <**Enter**>.

7. Move to cell **B8** and change the value to **43** by over-typing the original value. Press <Enter> and the formula in cell **F8** is instantly recalculated. A spreadsheet containing formulas is never out of date.

8. Leave the workbook open for the next Driving Lesson.

Driving Lesson 27 - Brackets

🅿 Park and Read

When more than one symbol is used in a formula, then the order becomes important, e.g. **A1+A2/A3**. *Excel* performs calculations in this order: **B**rackets over **D**ivision, **M**ultiplication, **A**ddition and finally **S**ubtraction (the **BODMAS** theory).

⟲ Manoeuvres

1. Click the **Sheet2** tab, ⟨ ⟨ ⟩ ⟩ Sheet1 **Sheet2** Sheet3 ⟩, (there is more than one worksheet in each workbook, clicking on a **Sheet** tab displays that sheet). Create the following small worksheet.

	A	B	C
1			
2	Sell Price	10	
3	Buy price	6	
4	Sold	4	
5	Profit		
6			

2. To calculate the profit, click on cell **B5** and type the formula **=B2-B3*B4** and press <**Enter**> to complete the formula.

3. The answer is given as **-14**, this is because multiplication is carried out before the subtraction, according to the **BODMAS** theory.

4. Click on cell **B5** and re-enter the formula, this time add the brackets around the subtraction part of the formula **=(B2-B3)*B4**, the old formula is replaced by the new.

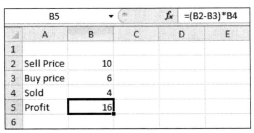

5. Check the answer displayed. Profit per item **10-6**, which is **4**, multiplied by the number sold, **4**, giving **16**.

6. Close the workbook <u>without</u> saving the changes.

ℹ️ *Brackets are added to force **Excel** to perform calculations in a different order. The calculation in the brackets will be performed first no matter what mathematical operation is used.*

Driving Lesson 28 - AutoSum

▣ Park and Read

The most common mathematical operation is addition. This calculation has been simplified by the use of a **Function** called **AutoSum**.

AutoSum can be found on two **Ribbon** tabs, **Home** and **Formulas**. The **Home** tab has a $\boxed{\Sigma \cdot}$ button in the **Editing** group and on the **Formulas** tab there is an **AutoSum** button, $\boxed{\Sigma \text{ AutoSum} \cdot}$, in the **Function Library** group.

AutoSum adds the contents of cells automatically.

⌐ Manoeuvres

1.   Start a new workbook.

2.   In the following cells, enter the following numbers:

▲	A	B	C	D	E
1					
2		2	1	3	
3		3	5	2	
4		4	2	1	
5					

3.   Click in cell **B5** and click the **AutoSum** button, $\boxed{\Sigma \text{ AutoSum} \cdot}$, on the **Formulas** tab, within the **Function Library** group.

▲	A	B	C	D	E
1					
2		2	1	3	
3		3	5	2	
4		4	2	1	
5		=SUM(B2:B4)			
6		SUM(**number1**, [number2], ...)			
7					

4.   Press <**Enter**> to complete the entry. The answer should be **9**.

5.   Repeat this in cells **C5** and **D5**.

6.   **AutoSum** also adds cells across. Click on cell **E2** and click the **AutoSum** button. Press <**Enter**> to complete the entry.

7.   Close the workbook <u>without</u> saving.

continued over

Driving Lesson 28 - Continued

8. Open the workbook **Sum**.

9. Select cell **B7**. The three numbers above need to be added together to find the number of apples sold in the three month period.

10. Click the **AutoSum** button,

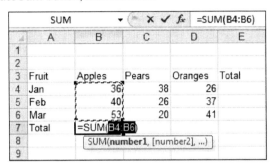

11. Finish the formula by pressing **<Enter>** to sum the numbers above. The answer should be **129**.

12. Move to cell **E4** and click the **AutoSum** button, [Σ AutoSum ▾]. The January figures are selected, press **<Enter>** to complete the formula. The answer should be **100**.

[i]   *AutoSum adds the cells above or left depending on where the figures are located. If AutoSum has figures in both directions it will sum the cells above by default, if no other formulas are involved.*

13. Use **AutoSum** to calculate the totals in cells, **C7**, **D7** and **E5**.

14. Use **AutoSum** to calculate the total in cell **E6**. After clicking [Σ AutoSum ▾] you will need to click and drag with the mouse from cell **B6** to cell **D6** to select the range **B6:D6**, as the cells above **E6** are selected by default.

15. Calculate the grand total in cell **E7** (adding cells to the left or above displays the same result, so the default range will be correct).

16. Save the workbook as **Sum Complete** and close it.

Driving Lesson 29 - Checking for Errors

▣ Park and Read

A worksheet is of little use if one formula within it is incorrect. Correct spelling is also important. It is vital that workbooks that are to be distributed are checked so that the worksheets contain no text or formula errors.

Formulas must be checked to see that they refer to the correct cells. Some formulas produce #**MESSAGE** denoting an error. Types of errors you need to recognise are:

#**DIV/0!**	Division by zero
#**REF!**	Cell referenced is not valid
#**NAME?**	Does not recognise text in a formula

You may also come across the following errors:

#**NULL!**	The two areas specified do not intersect
#**VALUE!**	The wrong argument used
#**NUM!**	Error with number in formula
#**N/A**	The value used in the formula is not available
######	The result is too long to fit into the cell

Typing and spelling mistakes can be checked either visually, or better still using *Excel's* spell checking facility. Corrections can then be made as appropriate.

⌐ Manoeuvres

1. Start a new workbook.

2. In cell **B3** type **6**, in cell **D3** type **8**, in cell **B5** type **10** and in cell **D5** enter the formula   **=B3+B5-D3**. Press <**Enter**>.

3. Double click on cell **D5** to check the formula.

SUM	▼	X ✓ *fx*	=B3+B5-D3	
	A	B	C	D	E
1					
2					
3		6		8	
4					
5		10		=B3+B5-D3	
6					

 Excel uses a different colour for each part of the formula.

4. If your screen matches the above diagram then it is correct. Press <**Enter**>.

5. Close the workbook <u>without</u> saving.

continued over

Driving Lesson 29 - Continued

6.   Open the workbook **Formulas**. Check the formulas on row **6** and cell **B12** for errors by double clicking on each cell. Remember to press <**Esc**> to cancel after checking.

7.   There is an error in cell **D6**, it contains a value, not a formula. Enter a formula in cell **D6** to multiply the two numbers above **=D4*D5**.

8.   Click on cell **E5** and enter **0**. The cell **E6** displays the **#DIV/0!** error message, division by zero. Click on cell **E6** and display the **Formulas** tab.

9.   Click the **Error Checking** button, [🔍 Error Checking ▾] in the **Formula Auditing** group. The error is described in the **Error Checking** dialog box. Read the information. Experiment with the options and then close It.

10. Close the workbook <u>without</u> saving.

11. Open the workbook **Spell**. With **A1** the active cell, click the **Review** tab and click the **Spelling** button, in the **Proofing** group.

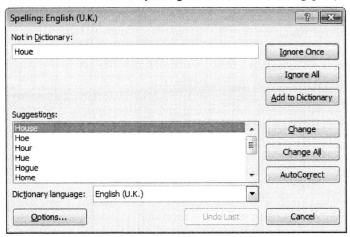

12. The **Spelling** dialog box will show the first mistake. **A1** is highlighted. The cell should read **House**. The **Suggestions** box displays **House**, click the **Change** button to correct the error.

13. The **Spelling** dialog box finds the next mistake in cell **A4**. The cell should read **Other**, the **h** has been missed out. Click on **Other** in the **Suggestions** list and then click the **Change** button. Correct the other mistakes on the worksheet.

[i] *Text can directly be entered into the **Change to** box if the required word is not in the **Suggestions** list or the error can be ignored.*

14. When finished spell checking, click **OK**.

15. Close the workbook <u>without</u> saving.

Driving Lesson 30 - Revision

This Driving Lesson covers the features introduced in this section. Try not to refer to the preceding Driving Lessons while completing it.

1.   On a blank worksheet enter the numbers in the cells to match below.

	A	B	C	D	E	F
1					4	
2					7	
3					5	
4					2	
5					4	
6					3	
7					8	
8					9	
9	8	2	4	7		
10						

2.   Click in cell **E9**. **AutoSum** is to be used. Will it sum the column or the row?

3.   Click the **AutoSum** button. Press <**Enter**>. What is the answer?

4.   Delete the answer in cell **E9** by clicking in cell **E9** and pressing the <**Delete**> key. You now need to sum the row of numbers. Click the **AutoSum** button, then click and drag from **A9** to **D9** or **D9** to **A9**. Press <**Enter**> to complete the formula. What is the answer?

5.   Click on cell **E3** and delete the contents.

6.   Delete the answer in **E9**.

7.   With cell **E9** active click the **AutoSum** button. You need to add all the column, click and drag the range **E1:E8**, press <**Enter**>. What is the answer?

8.   Close the workbook <u>without</u> saving it.

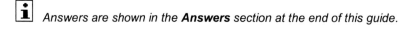

*Answers are shown in the **Answers** section at the end of this guide.*

If you experienced any difficulty completing this Revision refer back to the Driving Lessons in this section. Then redo the Revision.

Driving Lesson 31 - Revision

This Driving Lesson covers the features introduced in this section. Try not to refer to the preceding Driving Lessons while completing it.

1. Start a new workbook. The worksheet below contains data on boxes of fruit. Insert the following information in the cells indicated.

	A	B	C	D	E
1					
2					
3	Fruit	Apples	Pears	Oranges	Total
4	Jan	6	8	12	
5	Feb	7	6	10	
6	Mar	11	5	9	
7	Total				
8	Sell Price				
9	Income				
10	Buy Price				
11	Profit				
12					

2. Use **AutoSum** to sum the sales for each fruit (in **Row 7**) and for each month (in **Column E**). Calculate a grand total in cell **E7** (using either the column totals to the left or the row totals above).

3. The selling prices of the three fruits are **9**, **11** and **13** for the apples, pears and oranges respectively. Enter this information.

4. The **Income** row should contain formulas that multiply the **Total** by the **Sell Price**. Complete the three cells.

5. The buying prices of the three fruits are **5**, **6** and **7** for the apples, pears and oranges respectively. Enter this information.

6. The **Profit** is a more complicated formula, containing brackets. Work out the profit for one box of fruit using subtraction in brackets and multiply by the total number of boxes sold. The result in cell **B11** should be **96**.

7. Create similar formulas to calculate the profit for the pears and oranges.

8. Use **AutoSum** to calculate the total income in cell **E9** and total profit in cell **E11**. This should be **377**.

9. Check all the formulas by double clicking on each in turn and then save the completed workbook as **Fruit Sales** and close it.

If you experienced any difficulty completing this Revision refer back to the Driving Lessons in this section. Then redo the Revision.

Once you are confident with the features, complete the Record of Achievement Matrix referring to the section at the end of the guide. Only when competent move on to the next Section.

Section 5
Workbooks

By the end of this Section you should be able to:

Use Multiple Worksheets, Workbooks

Switch Between Open Workbooks

Rename Worksheets

Copy and Move Between Worksheets, Workbooks

Insert and Delete Worksheets

To gain an understanding of the above features, work through the **Driving Lessons** in this **Section**.

For each **Driving Lesson**, read the **Park and Read** instructions, without touching the keyboard, then work through the numbered steps of the **Manoeuvres** on the computer. Complete the **Revision Exercise(s)** at the end of the section to test your knowledge.

Driving Lesson 32 - Multiple Worksheets

🅿 Park and Read

A workbook can initially contain up to a maximum of 255 different worksheets, each with a different name. This allows related information to be kept together in the same workbook and complicated spreadsheet models to be created.

More than one workbook can open at the same time. This allows data, sheets and other objects to be copied or moved between workbooks.

ℝ Manoeuvres

1. Open the workbook **CIA**. This is a workbook containing **16** worksheets, representing a company with sixteen area divisions around the country.

2. Notice the sheet tabs across the bottom of the screen. Click on tab **Sheet3**. This makes the sheet active. All 16 sheets cannot be displayed because of the lack of space.

    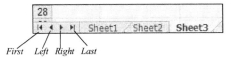

    First Left Right Last

3. There are 4 buttons to the left of **Sheet1** that control the sheet display. Click the **Last Sheet** button to switch to **Sheet16**. Click the sheet tab to make it active, the division name is in cell **B9**.

4. Move the divider between the tabs and the scroll bar to give more space to show more tabs.

    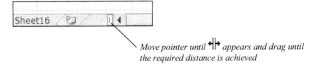

    Move pointer until ◀▮▶ appears and drag until the required distance is achieved

5. Practise using the sheet display buttons to view all the sheets.

6. Leave the workbook open for the next Driving Lesson.

ℹ️ *To adjust the number of sheets in a default workbook from **3**, click the **File** tab, then **Options** and from the **General** options settings, change the value in **Include this many sheets**. Click **OK**.*

Driving Lesson 33 - Switch Between Open Workbooks

▣ Park and Read

More than one workbook can be open at the same time. When a workbook is opened, it is displayed in the active window. Any previously opened workbooks are still open, but are hidden and not active.

↱ Manoeuvres

1. The **CIA** workbook should still be open. If not, open it. Open the workbook **Computer Sales**.

2. Remember, by default each workbook is displayed in the **Taskbar** on the **Excel** button. Click on the **Excel** button. The active book is highlighted.

3. Click **CIA** to make it active.

ⓘ *An alternative method to display a workbook is to click **Switch Windows** on the **View** tab. The open books are shown as a numbered list (the active book has a tick next to it). Selecting a name displays it.*

4. Open the workbook **Climate** and then open **Company**.

5. To display all open workbooks, click **Arrange All** found in the **Window** group on the **View** tab.

6. **Tiled** is the default, click **OK** to display all open books tiled. The four books are displayed. Use **Arrange All** to display each option in turn.

7. To display a single book, click the **Maximize** button of its window. Click on the **Climate** window and then maximise it. Maximising one, maximises all the windows.

8. Close **Climate**, then **Company**, then **Computer Sales**. Leave the **CIA** workbook open for the next Driving Lesson.

Driving Lesson 34 - Renaming Sheets

Park and Read

The names **Sheet1**, **Sheet2**, etc., are not very helpful for finding information. It makes much more sense to use meaningful names, which give a good idea of the content of the worksheet. The sheet tabs can contain up to **31** characters including spaces. Duplicate names are not allowed.

Manoeuvres

1.   The workbook **CIA** should still be open. If not, open it.

2.   To rename **Sheet1** as **North**, double click the **Sheet1** tab, the name **Sheet1** is highlighted.

3.   Type the new name **North**.

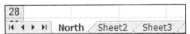

4.   Either press **<Enter>** or click on any cell on the sheet.

*An alternative method is to use the **Home** tab, **Format** button in the **Cells** group. Select **Rename Sheet**, enter the new name and press **<Enter>**.*

5.   Rename **Sheet2** as **North East**.

6.   Rename all the other sheets with the name of the **Division** in cell **B9**, using any method.

7.   Save the workbook as **Divisions**.

8.   Leave the workbook open for the next Driving Lesson.

Driving Lesson 35 - Copying and Moving Sheets

Park and Read

Sheets within a workbook can be moved or copied within the same, or to a different workbook.

Manoeuvres

1. The workbook **Divisions** should still be open. If not, open it.

2. Sheets can be moved and copied within the same workbook by dragging the sheet tab with the mouse. Move the **North Midlands** sheet between **South Wales** and **Midlands** by clicking and dragging to the correct position (a black triangle shows where the sheet will be inserted).

Use the Sheet scroll buttons to locate the sheets that are not visible.

3. Move the **North West** sheet to between **North** and **North East**.

4. A sheet is copied within the same workbook by holding <Ctrl> while dragging the sheet tab. To make a copy of the **North** sheet, hold down <Ctrl> then click and drag the **North** sheet tab across to the right, next to **North**. Release the mouse button first before <Ctrl>.

*The name of the copied sheet is **North (2)**. Duplicate sheet names are not allowed.*

5. If a sheet is to be moved or copied to another workbook the shortcut menu is used. Right click the **North (2)** sheet tab.

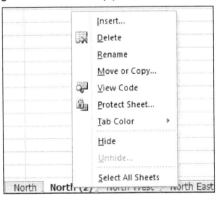

6. This menu controls all the actions relating to sheets. Select **Move or Copy**.

continued over

Driving Lesson 35 - Continued

7. To create a copy the **Create a copy** box is checked, otherwise the sheet is moved. Check the **Create a copy** box.

8. To move or copy to a different workbook, a selection is made from the **To book** box. Drop down the list to see the available open workbooks A new workbook is to be created to contain the copied sheet. Select **(new book)**.

*To move or copy to an existing workbook it must be open, so it is displayed in the **To book** box.*

9. The **Before sheet** box is empty for a new workbook. An existing one would display all the sheets for a selection to be made on the placement. Click **OK**.

10. A new workbook is created with just the sheet **North (2)** in it. Display the **Divisions** workbook and check that **North (2)** is still in this book and that it was copied.

11. Leave both workbooks open for the next Driving Lesson.

Driving Lesson 36 - Inserting and Deleting Sheets

▣ Park and Read

Once a workbook is open, sheets can be inserted or deleted to suit. The maximum number of sheets in a workbook is limited only by available memory.

⌒ Manoeuvres

1. Two workbooks, a new **Book** and **Divisions** are open from the previous Driving Lesson. The **South** division is to be closed because it is making vast losses. Right click the **South** tab in the **Divisions** workbook and select **Delete** from the shortcut menu.

2. Click **Delete** to complete the deletion.

 *An alternative method is to use the **Home** tab, **Delete** drop down in the **Cells** group. Select **Delete Sheet** and click **Delete**.*

3. The **Midlands** division is also doing poorly. Make **Midlands** active and delete it.

4. Sheets are inserted at the right of the current sheets. A new division called **Western** is to be created and it is to be located before the **Eastern** division. Click the **Insert Worksheet** button, [image], located to the right after the last sheet tab. A new sheet is inserted. Move the sheet to be before the **Eastern** sheet.

 *To insert a new worksheet the **Insert** drop down on the **Home** tab can be used. Select **Insert Sheet**. This command inserts a new worksheet to the left of the active sheet.*

5. Creating a new sheet similar to all the others will take too long. **Delete** the new sheet.

6. Make **Eastern** active and create a copy. The new sheet is named **Eastern (2)**. Rename the sheet and cell **B9** to **Western**.

7. Save the workbook **Divisions** using the same name and then close it.

8. Close the unsaved workbook <u>without</u> saving.

Driving Lesson 37 - Revision

This Driving Lesson covers the features introduced in this section. Try not to refer to the preceding Driving Lessons while completing it.

1. Open the workbook **Computer Sales**.

2. Delete the **Sales** sheet.

3. Copy the **Fruit** sheet to a new workbook.

4. Save the new workbook as **Copy** and then close it.

5. Insert a new sheet in **Computer Sales** ready to add more detailed information.

6. Rename the new sheet **Accounts**.

7. Display the **Fruit** sheet.

8. Save the workbook as **Computer Sales2**.

9. Close the workbook.

If you experienced any difficulty completing this Revision refer back to the Driving Lessons in this section. Then redo the Revision.

Once you are confident with the features, complete the Record of Achievement Matrix referring to the section at the end of the guide. Only when competent move on to the next.

Section 6
Editing

By the end of this Section you should be able to:

Edit Data in the Formula Bar and Cells

Delete Cell Contents

Use Undo and Redo

Select Ranges of Data

Use the Fill Handle

Erase and Sort Data

Cut, Copy and Paste

Find and Replace Text

To gain an understanding of the above features, work through the **Driving Lessons** in this **Section**.

For each **Driving Lesson**, read the **Park and Read** instructions, without touching the keyboard, then work through the numbered steps of the **Manoeuvres** on the computer. Complete the **Revision Exercise(s)** at the end of the section to test your knowledge.

Driving Lesson 38 - Editing Cells

P Park and Read

Changes can be made to data in cells in a variety of ways. The easiest way is to overtype one entry with another. When a cell entry is long or complicated small changes are either made in the **Formula Bar** or in the cell itself.

Manoeuvres

1. Open the workbook **CD Sales**.

2. Click the cell to be changed, in this case **B5**, **Quarters**.

3. Enter the new data label, **Months** to replace **Quarters**.

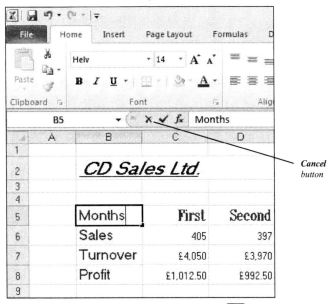

Cancel button

4. Before <**Enter**> is pressed, click the **Cancel** button, ☒, on the **Formula Bar**. This action cancels the new input, leaving the original data unchanged.

5. Click on cell **C8** and type in **Months**. This time press the **Escape** key <**Esc**>. This cancels the input and is quicker when typing. These methods to cancel are used when data is accidentally entered into the wrong cell. **C8** contains a formula to calculate the profit.

6. Type **Months** into cell **B5** again and press <**Enter**> to complete the entry. The new information replaces the old.

                                                                    continued over

Driving Lesson 38 - Continued

7.   Move into cell **B7**. Observe the cell contents in the **Formula Bar**. Click in the **Formula Bar** and change **Turnover** to **Income** using the **Backspace** key ⌫ (above <**Enter**>, make sure you don't use the left cursor key) to delete the text and type in **Income**. Press <**Enter**> to complete the change.

i   *When editing, the <**Enter**> key must be used to end the process.*

8.   In cell **B8** edit **Profit** to **Gross Profit**.

i   *The full label cannot be seen. Do not worry about this. Widening columns is covered in a later Driving Lesson.*

9.   Enter your first name in cell **A1** and complete the entry.

10. Double click in cell **A1**. A cursor is placed inside the cell to allow editing of the cell contents within the cell. If the cursor is not at the end of your first name, press the <**End**> key. Add a space and then your surname, press <**Enter**> to complete the entry.

11. Double click in cell **A1** to edit the contents. Click and drag to highlight your first name. Press the <**Delete**> key to remove it. Press <**Enter**> to leave just your surname in the cell.

12. Close the workbook **CD Sales** <u>without</u> saving.

Driving Lesson 39 - Deleting Cell Contents

P Park and Read

Excel allows the user to erase or delete data in many ways. Cell contents are erased using the **Clear Contents** command or by using <**Delete**> on the keyboard.

Manoeuvres

1. On a blank worksheet enter a number into cell **B4**. With **B4** selected erase the contents by clicking the **Clear** button, on the **Home** tab, **Editing** group. Select **Clear Contents**.

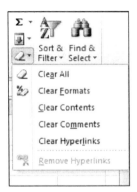

2. Enter any two numbers into cells **B2** and **B3**.

3. The **Delete** key can be used to clear contents. Select cell **B2** and then press <**Delete**>. The cell content is now cleared.

4. Clear the contents of cell **B3**.

5. Close the workbook <u>without</u> saving.

Driving Lesson 40 - Using Undo and Redo

⊞ Park and Read

As it is so easy to remove the contents of a cell, *Excel* has **Undo** to reverse any mistakes that may have been made. After undoing the action, it can be redone, if necessary, using **Redo**. The **Undo** and **Redo** buttons can be found on the **Quick Access Toolbar**.

⌒ Manoeuvres

1.   Open the workbook **CD Sales**.

2.   Click in cell **E6** and press <**Delete**> to remove the cell contents.

3.   Now delete the contents of cell **F6**.

4.   Click the **Undo** button, ⟲▾ , on the **Quick Access Toolbar**, to reverse the last action, i.e. put the contents back in **F6**.

ℹ️ *The exact wording displayed on the Tooltip after **Undo** is dependent on the action that has just been carried out.*

5.   Click the **Undo** button, ⟲▾ , to replace the deletion before last.

6.   After undoing an action, it can be redone by clicking the **Redo** button, ⟳▾ . Click the **Redo** button, ⟳▾ , to reverse the last action, the **Undo**.

7.   Use **Undo** to return the worksheet to its original state.

8.   Delete the contents of cells **B5**, **C5**, **D5**, **E5** and **F5** one at a time. All actions that can be undone are stored in the **Undo** history.

9.   To use this, click the drop down list next to the **Undo** button, ⟲▾ . Click and drag to **Clear** and **Undo 5 Actions**. The 5 deletions are restored.

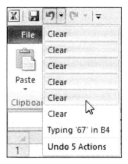

10.   Close the workbook **CD Sales** <u>without</u> saving the changes.

Driving Lesson 41 - Ranges

ⓟ Park and Read

A **range** is a rectangular selection of cells. Just as a single cell is identified by a cell reference, ranges are identified by the cells of their outer limits, e.g. the four cells B2, B3, C2 and C3 is the range **B2:C3**. Ranges are selected by clicking the mouse button and dragging to highlight a range of cells (known as **Click and Drag**).

Entire rows, columns, multiple rows, multiple columns and the entire worksheet can be selected using a similar technique.

Selections are made to allow the highlighted cells to be worked on, i.e. formatted, copied, moved, deleted, etc.

⌐ Manoeuvres

1. On a new worksheet click on cell **B2**. Click and drag down and to the right so that a range of six cells is highlighted, as shown below.

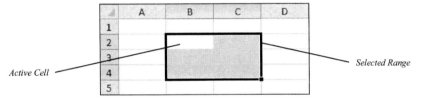

Active Cell   *Selected Range*

2. Release the mouse button. Notice that the first cell in the range remains white and the other cells are highlighted.

3. Selected ranges can be increased and decreased from the first cell in the range. Hold down the **<Shift>** key and select cell **E7**. The range is increased. Select cell **C2** while holding down **<Shift>** and the range is decreased. Click anywhere on the worksheet to remove the highlighted range.

4. Select the range **B2:C4** again. Press and hold down the **<Ctrl>** key. Click and drag the range **C5:D6**. Release the **<Ctrl>** key. There should now be two separate ranges highlighted. Click anywhere on the sheet to remove the selected ranges.

5. Click the **B** in the column border. Column **B** is now highlighted. Click on any cell to remove the selection.

6. Click on **5** in the row border. Row **5** is now highlighted. Click on any cell to remove the selection.

7. To select adjacent multiple columns, click in the column border and drag to select the required columns. Select columns **C** to **E**.

continued over

Driving Lesson 41 - Continued

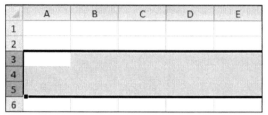

These diagrams have been captured running Excel in Windows 7.

8. To select multiple adjacent rows, click and drag in the row border. Click and drag from **3** to **5**. Several rows are highlighted.

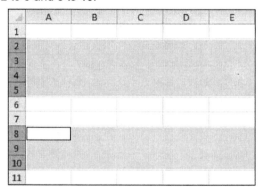

9. Click anywhere to remove the highlighting.

10. Non adjacent rows or columns can be selected using the same technique as for ranges, i.e. hold down the **<Ctrl>** key to select the separate part. Select rows **2** to **5** and **8** to **10**.

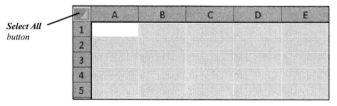

11. Select columns **B**, **C** and **E**.

12. To select the entire worksheet, click the **Select All** button (to the left of **A** and above **1**).

Select All button

13. Click on any cell to remove the highlighting.

Driving Lesson 42 - Using the Fill Handle

P Park and Read

The **Fill Handle** quickly copies or increments data to a range of cells. If the data is in the form of days, dates, time, months or text with a number then the **Fill Handle** will increment as it fills, otherwise the data will be copied.

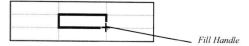

Fill Handle

i *It is only possible to drag in one direction at one time, i.e. across a row or down a column.*

Manoeuvres

1. On a blank worksheet enter your first name in **B2**.

2. Select **B2** and move the mouse pointer to the fill handle of **B2**. Click and drag the cell along to **G2**.

3. Your name will be copied into the cells and a **Smart Tag** will be displayed. Click the tag to see what options are available for this operation but do not select any.

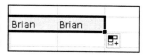

4. In **C4** enter **January**. Click and drag the fill handle of **C4** along to **G4**.

5. In **B6** enter today's date in the format **dd/mm/yyyy**.

6. Click and drag the fill handle of **B6** down to **B12**. The default is to increment each date by one day. Click the **Smart Tag** and select the **Fill Years** option. Each date is now incremented by one year.

7. Experiment using the fill handle with the following examples:

Mon	9:00 am	Order No 999
1-Jan	1st Quarter	Hello

8. Select tab **Sheet2** and enter **123** in cell **C3**. Click and drag the fill handle to cell **F3**. The entry **123** is repeated.

9. Select cell **C3** hold down the <Ctrl> key and click and drag with the fill handle to cell **C11**. The values are incremented.

10. In cell **B14** enter **10** and in cell **C14** enter **15**. Click and drag to highlight the range **B14:C14**. Use the **Fill Handle** for the selected range to click and drag to cell **H14**. The values are incremented by the original step (**5**).

11. Close the workbook <u>without</u> saving.

Driving Lesson 43 - Copying Cells

▣ Park and Read

Rather than repeatedly typing the same data into several cells, the **Copy** command can be used to copy labels, values and formulas. The selected cells are placed in an area of *Windows* called the **Clipboard**, from there they can be **Pasted** to other locations.

☞ Manoeuvres

1. On an empty worksheet, click on cell **B3**, type **Hello** then press **<Enter>**.

2. To copy this cell, click on cell **B3** and then click the **Copy** button, ▣▾.

i *The key press <**Ctrl C**> can be used instead of the **Copy** button,* ▣▾.

i *Excel places a **Marquee** (a moving dashed line) around the selected cell(s) to show which cells are to be copied. Notice that the message **Select destination and press ENTER or choose Paste** is displayed in the **Status Bar**.*

3. Move to cell **B7** and press **<Enter>**. The contents of **B3** will now be pasted into **B7**. The contents of **B3** will remain unchanged. Note that **B3** no longer has a dashed line around it.

4. Enter **65** into cell **C6** and with cell **C6** active, click the **Copy** button.

5. Move to **B9** and click the **Paste** button. The value is pasted into the new location and a **Smart Tag**, ▣ (Ctrl) ▾ is displayed.

6. Click the tag to see a list of options concerning the pasting process. Do not select any.

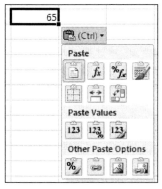

i *The key press <**Ctrl V**> can be used instead of the **Paste** button.*

continued over

Driving Lesson 43 - Continued

7.   Note that **C6** still has a dashed line, indicating that its contents can be pasted again if required. Move to **B10** and paste again. Press **<Esc>** to end the pasting and remove the dashed line around **C6**.

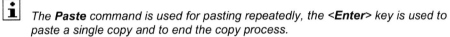

*The **Paste** command is used for pasting repeatedly, the **<Enter>** key is used to paste a single copy and to end the copy process.*

8.   Select the **Clipboard** group launcher to display the **Clipboard Task Pane** if not already shown. The clipboard is common to all *Office* applications, so it may contain many items already. Click [**Clear All**] to remove any existing items.

9.   To copy a range, highlight the range **B7:B10** and click the **Copy** button. The values will appear in the **Clipboard Task Pane**.

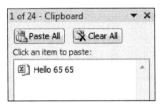

10. As well as using the **Paste** button or the **<Enter>** key, items can be pasted directly from the **Clipboard**. Click the destination cell, **H5**, which will become the top left cell of the pasted range and then click the entry in the **Clipboard** to paste the range.

11. Cells can be copied from sheet to sheet within the same book and can be pasted more than once from the **Clipboard**.

12. Click the **Sheet3** tab at the bottom of the worksheet area to display that sheet.

13. Click on cell **A2** and then click the entry in the **Clipboard** to paste the range. The four cells from **Sheet1** are copied to **Sheet3**.

14. Click back on **Sheet1** to check that the original range is still present.

15. Close the workbook <u>without</u> saving.

Driving Lesson 44 - Moving Cells

 Park and Read

The **Cut** and **Paste** commands allow the user to <u>move</u> the content of a cell or a range of cells to other parts of the worksheet, other worksheets or other workbooks.

Care should be taken when moving numbers into cells that are referenced by formulas.

 Manoeuvres

1. Start a new workbook.

2. Enter any two numbers in **E5** and **E6**. In **E7** enter a formula to add the two numbers.

3. Select the range **E5:E6**. Click the **Cut** button, ✂, to cut the selected cells from the worksheet (they are still there at this point until pasted).

 *The key press <**Ctrl X**> can be used instead of the **Cut** button.*

4. Move the pointer to **G7** and click the **Paste** button. The values appear in the new location and disappear from the original cells, i.e. they are moved.

5. Notice that the calculation in **E7** is still correct. Click on cell **E7** to see that the calculation now references the new locations.

 *Remember that the key press <**Ctrl V**> can be used instead of the **Paste** button.*

6. In **C8** enter the formula **=C6+C7**, the cell should display zero.

7. Select cell **G7** and **G8**, click with the right mouse button and select **Cut** from the shortcut menu.

8. Move to cell **C6** right click, and select **Paste.** The result calculated now shows **#REF!** an error message.

 Take care when pasting into cells that contain data as the original information is overwritten. If cells are referenced by formulas those cells are shown as errors.

9. Click the **Undo** button to reverse the last paste. Press <**Esc**> to remove the marquee.

continued over

Driving Lesson 44 - Continued

10. In cell **G9** use **AutoSum** to add the two numbers (there is an **AutoSum**, button. $\boxed{\Sigma \cdot}$, in the **Editing** group on the **Home** tab). These three cells can be cut or copied and pasted on the same sheet.

11. Highlight the range **G7:G9** and select to **Cut**.

12. Click on cell **B3** and use **Paste** to place the three cells. Click on cell **B5** and note the formula references the two cells directly above.

i   *Cells or ranges that are **Cut** also appear on the **Clipboard** as with the **Copy** function, but if they are pasted from there, the original entries are NOT removed from the **Clipboard**.*

13. As well as moving cells on the same sheet they can also be moved between sheets in the same book. Highlight the range **B3:B5** and click **Cut**.

14. Select the **Sheet2** tab, click on cell **H4** and click **Paste**. The cell contents are removed from **Sheet1** and placed on **Sheet2**. Check both **Sheet1** and **Sheet2**.

15. Close the **Clipboard** by clicking the **Close** button.

16. On **Sheet1** delete the cell contents of cell **C8** and **E7**. The sheet should now be blank.

17. Close the open workbook without saving.

Driving Lesson 45 - Copying & Moving between Workbooks

▣ Park and Read

The cells can also be copied or moved from workbook to workbook.

☞ Manoeuvres

1. Open the workbooks **League** (world hockey leagues) and **Survey** (an analysis of 220 hockey fans and whether they replied to a survey).

2. A sample of 20 people from the survey has been requested. In the **Survey** workbook, highlight the range from **A:G** of 20 rows from anywhere in the survey and select to **Copy** using any method.

3. Click **Switch Windows** from the **View** tab and click **League** from the drop down list to display the **League** workbook. Alternatively, click the workbook name **League** on the **Taskbar** to display that workbook.

4. Click on the **Sheet2** tab.

5. Click on cell **C5** (the cell to place the copy) and then press **<Enter>**. The range is copied from **Survey** to **Sheet2** in the **League** workbook.

ⓘ *The data is not fully displayed because the columns are not wide enough. The widening of columns is covered later. Leave it for now.*

6. Make **Survey** the active workbook and close it <u>without</u> saving.

ⓘ *Single cells are copied from sheet to sheet and book to book in exactly the same way as a range.*

ⓘ *The Clipboard can also be used to copy and paste information between any Microsoft Office applications.*

7. Not only can cells be moved between sheets they can be moved between workbooks. Display the workbook **League, Sheet1**. Highlight the range **A32:I50** (the last 2 leagues). Select to **Cut**.

8. Start a new workbook and on **Sheet1** make the active cell **A2** and **Paste** the cells. This moves the cells to a different workbook.

9. View the workbook **League**, to see if the data has been removed from **Sheet1**.

10. Copy the contents of **A1** (the title) and select the new workbook. Paste the copied contents in **A1**. Left align the label text.

11. Save the new workbook as **Lower Leagues** and close it. Close the workbook **League** <u>without</u> saving.

Driving Lesson 46 - Finding Specific Text

🅿 Park and Read

Specific text can be found in formulas, labels, comments, etc. and even replaced if necessary. The search starts at the active cell.

🏴 Manoeuvres

1. Open the workbook **Hotel**.

2. With **A1** the active cell and the **Home** tab displayed, click the **Find & Select** button in the **Editing** group. Select **Find**.

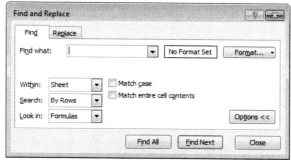

> ℹ️ *If the options are not displayed, click the **Options** button to display them. Options include whether to search by row or column, whether the text is part or all of the cell content, and whether the text case is important. Make sure all settings are as shown here.*

3. In the **Find what** box, enter **Daily Rate** and click on **Find Next**.

4. The active cell will now be **R3**, the **Daily Rate**.

> ℹ️ *It may be necessary to move the **Find and Replace** dialog box so that the results of the search can be seen.*

5. Close the **Find and Replace** dialog box and use the key press <**Ctrl Home**> to move to cell **A1**.

6. Find **Tax**. Select **By Rows** in the **Search** box, if not already selected. Click on **Find Next**.

7. The active cell will be **Q22**, the **Tax Rates** label. To find any other occurrences of **Tax**, click on **Find Next**.

8. The active cell is now **A36**, the **Company Tax**. Click **Find Next**. There should be no others. **Close** the dialog box.

9. Leave the workbook open as it is used in the next Driving Lesson.

Driving Lesson 47 - Replacing Text

▣ Park and Read

In a similar manner to finding text, it can be found then replaced.

↱ Manoeuvres

1.   Use **Hotel**, with **A1** the active cell, click the **Find & Select** button in the **Editing** group. Select **Replace**. Ensure that the full version of the dialog box is displayed. Click **Options** if necessary.

2.   In the **Find what** box, enter **room** and in **Replace with**, enter **chamber**.

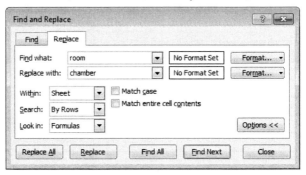

3.   Click on **Find Next**. The first occurrence of **room** is highlighted. It may be necessary to move the **Replace** dialog box so that the affected cell can be seen.

4.   Click on **Replace** to change it to **chamber**. Continue clicking **Replace** to change all of the rooms to chambers. When all are replaced a message dialog box is displayed.

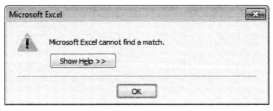

5.   Click **OK**.

6.   In the **Find what** box, enter **chamber**, and in **Replace with** enter **room**. Ensure that **Match case** is not checked and select **Replace All**.

7.   All occurrences of **chamber** have now been replaced with **room**. Click **OK** at the confirmation message. Close the **Replace** dialog box.

8.   Close the workbook <u>without</u> saving.

Driving Lesson 48 - Sorting

🅿 Park and Read

In a list, the rows can be arranged in a specific order using the column headings, C, D, etc., or column titles, e.g. a header row or labels, as a reference. The **Sort A to Z** button, | A↓ Sort A to Z | and the **Sort Z to A** button, | Z↓ Sort Z to A |, are used to sort text. The button text changes to **Sort Smallest to Largest** and **Sort Largest to Smallest** when sorting numbers. The rows are sorted automatically on the column containing the active cell.

The **Sorting** commands can be found on two **Ribbon** tabs, **Home** and **Data**. The **Home** tab has a **Sort & Filter** button in the **Editing** group and on the **Data** tab there is a **Sort & Filter** group containing the buttons.

⌒ Manoeuvres

1. Start a new workbook.

2. Enter a column of 8 names (surnames or first names) starting in cell **B3**.

3. Sort the names into ascending alphabetic order, click in an occupied cell in column **B**. On the **Home** tab select **Sort & Filter** in the **Editing** group and then click the **Sort A to Z** button, | A↓ Sort A to Z |.

4. With the active cell still in column **B** use the same menu but click the **Sort Z to A** button, | Z↓ Sort Z to A |. The names are sorted into descending order.

5. Add ages (in years) in column **C** adjacent to the names.

6. To sort the ages list into ascending order, click in an occupied cell in column **C**. Display the **Data** tab and click | A↓ | in the **Sort & Filter** group. The ages are sorted in ascending order with the names in column **B** kept with correct ages.

7. Sort the ages into descending order.

ℹ *More complicated sorting can be carried out using the **Custom Sort** command, using the **Sort** dialog box.*

8. Close the workbook <u>without</u> saving.

Driving Lesson 49 - Revision

This Driving Lesson covers the features introduced in this section. Try not to refer to the preceding Driving Lessons while completing it.

1. Open the workbook **Home Finances**.

2. Examine your finances to decide whether you can afford to buy a new camera, costing £90, for your holiday in August. Go to cell **N16** and look at your total savings for the end of the year. They are estimated to be less than you need to buy that camera, so drastic action is needed if you do not want to owe money at the end of the year.

3. From the beginning of January you decide to stop using your car and save petrol by cycling to work for three months. Select the range of cells for **Petrol** expenses from **Jan** through to **Mar**. As you feel extremely health conscious you decide to extend your cycling through to July, use the <**Shift**> key to extend the range to **Jul** and clear the cell contents.

4. Check **N16**. How much savings do you now have?

5. This good news is short lived as you realise that you do not own a bike and will have to continue to use the car. Click the **Undo** button to put the figures for your petrol back into the worksheet.

6. You now decide to limit your **Leisure** expenses to a maximum of £50 per month from **Jan** through to **Jul**. Type **50** in **Jan Leisure** (cell **B7**) and use the fill handle to copy this through to **Jul**.

	A	B	C	D	E	F	G	H	I
1	*House Finance*	Jan	Feb	Mar	Apr	May	Jun	Jul	Aug
2	Pay	415	415	415	415	415	415	415	415
3	Other Income	0	0	0	0	0	0	0	0
4	Total Income	415	415	415	415	415	415	415	415
5	Rent	80	80	80	80	80	80	80	90
6	Holidays	0	0	0	50	0	0	0	210
7	Leisure	50	50	50	50	50	50	50	187
8	Electricity	49	0	0	43	0	0	29	0
9	Gas	46	0	0	51	0	0	32	0
10	Telephone	0	37	0	0	35	0	0	36

7. Check **N16**, how much have you now saved?

8. You intend to purchase the camera in July so add **90** to the figure already in **Others** for July.

9. How much will you have in your savings by the end of the year now?

10. Close the workbook <u>without</u> saving.

i

*Answers are shown in the **Answers** section at the end of this guide.*

If you experienced any difficulty completing this Revision refer back to the Driving Lessons in this section. Then redo the Revision.

Driving Lesson 50 - Revision

This Driving Lesson covers the features introduced in this section. Try not to refer to the preceding Driving Lessons while completing it.

1. Create a blank spreadsheet. Enter **February** in **B2**, **Week 1** in **C3** and **Mon** in **B4**. Use the **Fill Handle** to produce the following sheet.

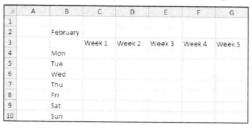

2. The first day of **February 2008** was a **Friday**. Type **01/02/08** into cell **C8**. By default, dates are displayed in the format, **01/02/2008**. Use the **Fill Handle** to drag **C8** to **C10**.

3. Enter **04/02/08** in cell **D4**, **11/02/08** in cell **E4**, **18/02/08** in cell **F4 and 25/02/08** in cell **G4**.

4. Fill the blank days of the week using the **Fill Handle**. What day of the week was the last day of **February** and was **2008** a leap year?

5. In cell **B13** type **Year**. In cell **B14** type the year you were born, e.g. **1983**.

6. Use the **<Ctrl>** key to fill the cells below **B14** by dragging down the column until the series of dates reaches the present year.

7. In cell **C13** type **Age** and in cell **C14** type **0**, as you were born in that year.

8. Fill the column down increasing the series by **1** each time until you reach the current year. You should now see how old you will be this year.

9. In cell **D13** type **Days Old**. In cell **D14** type **0** and in **D15** type **365**. Highlight the two numbers and use the **Fill Handle** to fill down the column. Remember that this is an approximate figure as no account is taken for leap years.

10. Continue to increase the series in column **C** until **65**. Increase column **B** and **D** also to match column **C**. How many days old will you be or were you when **65** years old?

11. Close the workbook <u>without</u> saving.

If you experienced any difficulty completing this Revision refer back to the Driving Lessons in this section. Then redo the Revision.

Once you are confident with the features, complete the Record of Achievement Matrix referring to the section at the end of the guide. Only when competent move on to the next Section.

Section 7
Printing

By the end of this Section you should be able to:

Print a Worksheet and Workbook

Use Print Preview

Change the Page Setup

Add Headers and Footers

Use Print Titles

Display and Print Formulas

Print Specified Areas of a Worksheet

To gain an understanding of the above features, work through the **Driving Lessons** in this **Section**.

For each **Driving Lesson**, read the **Park and Read** instructions, without touching the keyboard, then work through the numbered steps of the **Manoeuvres** on the computer. Complete the **Revision Exercise(s)** at the end of the section to test your knowledge.

Driving Lesson 51 - Printing

▣ Park and Read

Worksheets can be printed out to give a hard copy. It is possible to decide what to print: the sheet, the pages and the number of copies.

It is customary to **Print Preview** the worksheet before printing, as it may not fit on the paper, as you need it to.

Manoeuvres

1. Open the workbook **Company**. This is a small worksheet and therefore fits easily on one piece of paper.

    ⓘ *Make sure that the appropriate printer is attached to your computer and that it is switched on and is on-line before attempting to print.*

2. Click the **File** tab, select **Print** or use the key press <**Ctrl P**> to display the **Print** options screen. The left-hand side controls what is printed. The right-hand side shows a preview.

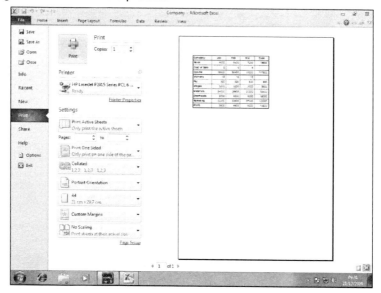

3. The default settings are to print the **Active sheets** and **1** for the **Copies**. Click the **Print** button to print one copy of the worksheet.

4. All the worksheets in a workbook can be printed. Click the **File** tab and then **Print**. Click the **Print Active Sheets** drop down and select **Print Entire Workbook** and click the **Print** button. The two sheets are printed.

5. Close the workbook <u>without</u> saving.

Driving Lesson 52 - Print Preview

🅿 Park and Read

In this version of *Excel* print preview is integrated into the **Print** options screen. The preview is shown on the right. The preview shows the layout of the worksheet on the page(s). **Page Setup** can be activated from here by clicking the **Page Setup** link. This link is used to perform tasks that are not available from the **Print** options screen, e.g. controlling **Headers and Footers**.

☞ Manoeuvres

1. Open the workbook **Exam Results**. Click the **File** tab and click the **Print** option.

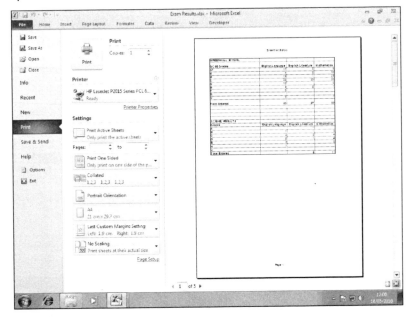

2. The preview on the right shows how the worksheet will be printed. The worksheet covers five pages. Look at the bottom of the preview it displays, ◄ 1 of 5 ►. Click the right arrow; **Next Page** to view the second page.

3. The **Next Page** and **Previous Page** arrows are used to view the rest of the pages of the multi-page worksheet. This is a five page document. Return to **Page 1**.

ℹ️ *The scroll bar can be used to display the pages of a multi-page worksheet.*

4. Leave the workbook open for the next Driving Lesson.

Driving Lesson 53 - Page Setup

▣ Park and Read

Page Setup is used to change the way a worksheet is displayed on the pages. Pages can be printed in either **Portrait** or **Landscape** view or can be scaled to fit on a number of pages. However, many of these features can now be controlled within the **Print** options screen under **Settings**.

☞ Manoeuvres

1. Use the workbook **Exam Results**.

2. Click the **File** tab and click the **Print** option. Take note that there are **5** pages.

3. The page settings are controlled via the **Settings** options listed on the left.

4. Click the **Portrait Orientation** option and select **Landscape Orientation**.

5. There are now three pages, notice that **Landscape** is where the largest edge of the paper is across the top. Use the **Next Page** and **Previous Page** arrows to view all the pages.

continued over

Driving Lesson 53 - Continued

6.   To fit the worksheet to a set number of pages the **Scaling** option is used. Click the No Scaling option and select the **Fit Sheet on One Page** option. The worksheet will be fitted on a single page. Select to fit the worksheet onto a single page. It may be a little difficult to read.

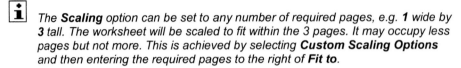 *The **Scaling** option can be set to any number of required pages, e.g. **1** wide by **3** tall. The worksheet will be scaled to fit within the 3 pages. It may occupy less pages but not more. This is achieved by selecting **Custom Scaling Options** and then entering the required pages to the right of **Fit to**.*

7.   Click the **Fit Sheet on One Page** and select **No Scaling** to return the worksheet to its previous setting of 3 pages.

8.   The default **Paper size** is **A4**, but this can be changed if working with different sized paper. Click the **A4** option.

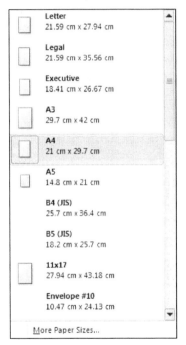

 *The actual **Paper size** options available will depend on the model of printer in use.*

9.   Examine the list and then select **A5**. The worksheet is now on 10 pages.

10.   Change the paper size back to **A4**.

11.   Leave the workbook open for the next Driving Lesson.

Driving Lesson 54 - Margins

▣ Park and Read

Margins can be reduced or enlarged to give more or less white space around a worksheet. Margins are normally reduced to allow more of a worksheet to fit on each piece of paper.

⌐ Manoeuvres

1. Using the workbook **Exam Results,** in the **Print** options, select **Custom Margins**.

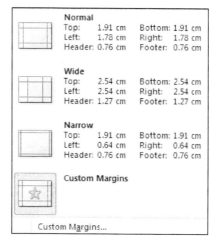

2. This displays only limited options, **Normal**, **Wide** and **Narrow**. If one of these is suitable then select it. For more control click the **Custom Margins** text at the bottom of the list.

3. The **Page Setup** dialog box is displayed. To change **Margin** settings (values are in centimetres), either type in the values or use ⬍ to increase or decrease the values within the **Top**, **Bottom**, **Left** and **Right** boxes. The worksheet is **Landscape** and fits across three pages; reduce the **Left** margin down to **0.4** by clicking in the box and changing the amount.

4. Change the **Right** margin down to **0.4** by clicking three times on the down spinner (the down triangle).

5. Clicking in the **Center on page** boxes centres the worksheet horizontally and/or vertically. Check the **Vertically** option. Click **OK** to accept the changes. There are now only two pages, with the worksheet centred vertically on each page.

6. Close **Exam Results**, click **Don't Save** to close <u>without</u> saving.

Driving Lesson 55 - Printing a Selection

🅿 Park and Read

It is possible to print just a part of a worksheet, a selected range for example. You might want to do this when only a small area of the worksheet is relevant for your intended audience.

↱ Manoeuvres

1. Open the workbook **Hotel**.

2. Select the range **A3:E17,** i.e. the first four months of receipts.

3. Click the **File** tab and then **Print** or use the key press <**Ctrl P**> to display the **Print** options screen.

4. Click **Print Active Sheets** and select the **Print Selection**.

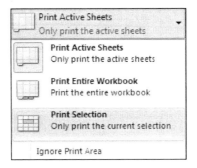

5. Click the **Print** button to print the selection.

6. Close the workbook <u>without</u> saving.

Driving Lesson 56 - Headers and Footers

🅿 Park and Read

Headers and **Footers** are lines of text which appear at the top/bottom of every printed page. They can contain text or field codes in the three areas: **Left section**, **Center section** and **Right section**.

🗗 Manoeuvres

1. Open the workbook **League**. This is a workbook that contains various hockey leagues, similar to the World Cup in football.

2. Display the **Insert** tab and click the **Header & Footer** button. This displays the **Header** on the worksheet and the **Design** tab within **Header & Footer Tools**. The view is **Page Layout**.

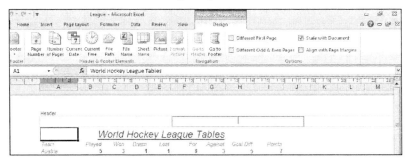

3. Examine the **Design** tab to see the available tools when dealing with **Headers and Footers**.

4. The cursor is placed in the central section. Type the title **World Hockey Tables**. Any text can be entered by typing in any of the sections; left, centre or right.

5. Place the cursor in the **Right section** and type **Provisional**.

ℹ️ *There are various buttons on the **Design** tab that place field codes into **Headers** and **Footers** and these are covered when adding a **Footer**.*

6. Scroll down the worksheet to see the header on both pages. The title on row 1 of the worksheet is now duplicated by the **Header** on page one.

ℹ️ *When adding a title choose between using a cell on the worksheet or a **Header**.*

7. Click on the **Header** and edit the centre text to **World Hockey League Tables**. Delete the text in the right section to remove it.

continued over

Driving Lesson 56 - Continued

8. The title on row 1 is now surplus. Click on cell **A1** and remove the cell's contents.

9. Click in the header. Display the **Design** tab and click the **Go to Footer** button, to display the blank footer.

10. Click in the **Left section** and then click the **Current Date** button, this places the field code **&[Date]** in the box. This code displays the current date. Add a space and then click the **Current Time** button, to add the current time. The codes are displayed, &[Date] &[Time] .

11. Click in the **Center section**. The left section now displays the codes as text, e.g. 24/05/2010 10:12 .

12. Type **Page** (followed by a space) and click the **Page number** button, . *Excel* places the field code **&[Page]** in the box.

13. Click in the **Right section** and click the **Sheet Name** button, , press / and then click the **File Name** button, . The field codes are **&[Tab]** and **&[File]**. This identifies the printout, it displays the sheet and book names.

14. Scroll the worksheet to check each part of the **Footer**. Check both pages.

i *To delete a field in a **Header/Footer**, select the field code and press <Delete>.*

15. The worksheet has two pages in **Landscape** view. Display the **Page Layout** tab, click the **Orientation** button and select **Portrait**. The worksheet should only be one page.

16. To change the view back to normal display the **View** tab and click the **Normal** button.

i *Click the **Page Layout** button on the **View** tab to show the headers and footers on the worksheet.*

17. Save the workbook as **League2** and close it.

i *Headers and footers can also be created and edited using the **Header/Footer** tab within the **Page Setup** dialog box.*

Driving Lesson 57 - Print Titles

▣ Park and Read

Rows and columns of the worksheet may be specified as titles, and these can be displayed on each printed page. This is often used to show labels on each page.

↷ Manoeuvres

1. Open the workbook **Survey**.

2. Display the **Page Layout** tab and click the **Print Titles** button.

3. The **Page Setup** dialog box showing the **Sheet** tab is displayed.

4. Click in the **Rows to repeat at top** box, click the **Collapse** button, and select rows **1** to **5** (the dialog box may have to be moved to do this). Click to expand the dialog box.

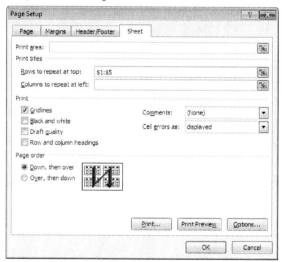

5. Click **OK**.

6. Click the **File** tab and then **Print**. Use the **Next Page** arrow to see the other pages. Notice that the first five rows of the worksheet are repeated on every page.

ℹ️ *Columns to repeat at left can be set for worksheets that are short and wide. Both rows and columns cannot be set as **Print titles** at the same time.*

7. Close the workbook <u>without</u> saving.

ℹ️ *Print titles <u>cannot</u> be set using **Page Setup** from within **Print** options.*

Driving Lesson 58 - Displaying & Printing Formulas

▣ Park and Read

Instead of formula results, the actual formulas themselves can be displayed on screen and then printed. This is useful when checking that formulas are correct.

↱ Manoeuvres

1. Open the workbook **Formulas**, which contains some simple calculations.

2. Enter **6** in cell **B4**. Is the answer correct in **B6**? Click on cell **B6**. Check the **Formula Bar** for the formula.

3. To display all the formulas on the screen, click **Show Formulas** ▥ Show Formulas from the **Formulas** tab. The formulas are now shown.

ℹ *Alternatively, and much more quickly, it is possible to switch between formulas and their results by pressing* **<Ctrl `>**, *i.e.* **Ctrl** *and the key to the left of 1.*

4. Switch to the results and then switch back to the formulas using the quick key press method.

5. There is a problem with cell **D6**, it contains the number **10**. Enter the formula to multiply the two numbers **=D4*D5**.

6. If the formulas are to be printed, it is normal to display the row and column headings and the gridlines with the formulas so they can be checked. Display the **Page Layout** tab and then check **Print** under **Gridlines** and **Print** under **Headings**, in the **Sheet Options** group.

7. Use **Print options** to preview the results.

8. On the **Page Layout** tab uncheck **Print** under **Gridlines** and **Print** under **Headings** to stop the **Headings** and **Gridlines** from being printed.

9. Click the **Show Formulas** button on the **Formulas** tab to remove the displayed formulas.

10. Close the workbook <u>without</u> saving.

Driving Lesson 59 - Revision

This Driving Lesson covers the features introduced in this section. Try not to refer to the preceding Driving Lessons while completing it.

1.   Open the workbook **Oscars**.

2.   Add a centred header **Oscar Winners** and insert page numbering in the right section of the footer.

3.   Change the page orientation to **Landscape**.

4.   Change the top and bottom, margins to **2.0**.

5.   Change the left and right margins to **0.4**.

6.   Select and print the last 10 Oscar winning films only.

7.   Change the **Print Titles** to repeat row 1 on all the pages.

8.   Print a copy of the entire worksheet.

9.   Close the workbook <u>without</u> saving.

If you experienced any difficulty completing this Revision refer back to the Driving Lessons in this section. Then redo the Revision.

Driving Lesson 60 - Revision

This Driving Lesson covers the features introduced in this section. Try not to refer to the preceding Driving Lessons while completing it.

1. Open the workbook **Hotel**.

2. Alter the page settings for printing to the following:

    Header -   Change to **Company Finances** (centred)

    Footer -   Remove the word **Page** to leave just the page number

    Margins -   **Top** and **Bottom** to **2cm** and **Left** and **Right** to **1cm**

3. Print out **Page 2** only.

4. Using **Page Titles**, select to repeat **Column A**.

5. Select the range **F3:J14** and print the selection.

6. Close the workbook <u>without</u> saving.

7. Open the workbook **Company**. This is a small workbook containing two worksheets, **Actual** and **Forecast**.

8. The worksheets are very similar and it is difficult to identify which is which from the printed copies. Add a centred **Sheet Name** code to each of the worksheets in the footer.

9. Print a copy of the entire workbook.

10. Close the **Company** workbook <u>without</u> saving.

If you experienced any difficulty completing this Revision refer back to the Driving Lessons in this section. Then redo the Revision.

Once you are confident with the features, complete the Record of Achievement Matrix referring to the section at the end of the guide. Only when competent move on to the next Section.

Section 8
Formatting

By the end of this Section you should be able to:

Format Numbers, Dates & Percentages

Change Cell Alignment and Rotate Text

Add Borders and Colour

Change Row Height and Column Width

Insert and Delete Rows and Columns

Use Freeze & Zoom

Use the Format Painter

To gain an understanding of the above features, work through the **Driving Lessons** in this **Section**.

For each **Driving Lesson**, read the **Park and Read** instructions, without touching the keyboard, then work through the numbered steps of the **Manoeuvres** on the computer. Complete the **Revision Exercise(s)** at the end of the section to test your knowledge.

Driving Lesson 61 - Formatting

🅿 Park and Read

To **Format** is to change the way cells look in order to improve the overall appearance of a worksheet. The **Home** tab is used to achieve the full range of formatting.

Formatting can change the style, size, colour, alignment and number format of text and numbers, the border style, colour and pattern of cells.

🖙 Manoeuvres

1. Open the workbook **Climate**.

2. Display the **Home** tab and click **Format** in the **Cells** group. Select **Format Cells**. The cells to be formatted would normally be selected before using this command, but it is used here for observation only.

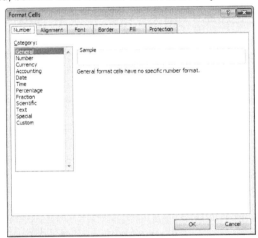

3. The **Format Cells** dialog box is displayed. This is a six tabbed dialog box.

4. The **Number** tab is the first, if this is not displayed, click **Number**. This tab controls the way numbers are shown, including dates and times.

5. Click **Alignment**, this positions information in cells. Click **Font**, this changes the text style, size and other text features.

6. Click **Border**, this controls the lines around the cells. Click **Fill**, this controls background cell colour. Click **Protection**, this is part of a system to stop information being lost.

7. Click **Cancel** to close the **Format Cells** dialog box.

8. Leave the workbook open for the next Driving Lesson.

Driving Lesson 62 - Bold, Underline & Italic

Park and Read

The easiest way to make a cell stand out is to make it **Bold**. This works well with titles.

Underline is a line under the cell contents (not a cell border).

Italic gives you leaning text, similar to handwriting.

Manoeuvres

1. Using the workbook **Climate**, select the cells **B2:J2**.

2. To make this range of cells **Bold**, click the **Bold** button, **B**, in the **Font** group.

> The button is displayed with a different background to show when the feature is active. This applies to all the formatting buttons.

3. Select the cells **A2:A18** and click once on the following buttons, **Italic**, *I* and **Underline**, U .

> The **Underline** button has a drop down arrow with a **Double Underline** option. After applying a double underline the button changes to D

4. Click anywhere on the worksheet to remove the highlighted selection and see the results. The underlining of a column of labels is not very effective.

5. Select cells **A2:A18** again and click the **Underline** button, U , again to turn off the underlining. Click anywhere on the worksheet to remove the highlighted section.

6. There are quick key presses for bold, italic and underline. Click on cell **A2**. Press <**Ctrl B**> to add **Bold**, and to add **Underline**, press <**Ctrl U**>. The key press for **Italic** is <**Ctrl I**>, this cell already has **Italic** added.

7. The same keys turn off the formatting. Press <**Ctrl I**> and <**Ctrl U**> to turn off italic and underline for cell **A2**.

> The **Font** tab within the **Format Cells** dialog box could have been used to apply this formatting but the buttons and key presses are quicker.

8. To double underline the contents of cell **A2**, click the drop down on the **Underline** button in the **Font** group and select **Double Underline**.

9. Leave the workbook open for the next Driving Lesson.

Driving Lesson 63 - Fonts & Font Size

P Park and Read

A **Font** is a type or style of print. Examples of fonts are Arial, Times New Roman, Modern, **Script**, etc. The default font and font size is **Calibri 11**. **Font Size** is measured in points, more points means a larger size.

Manoeuvres

1. Use the workbook **Climate**.

2. Select cell **A2**, the title. To change the font, a selection can be made using the **Font** drop down (the down triangle) in the **Font** group, `Arial ▾`. As the mouse moves over each font the results are displayed on the worksheet.

3. Change the font to **Algerian** (if not available, any other font).

4. Highlight the range **B2:J2** and change the font to **Times New Roman** (scroll down the font list to find the required one).

5. To make the titles bigger you can change the **Font Size**. Select cell **A2** and change the size by clicking on the drop down **Font Size** box, `10 ▾`, in the **Font** group.

6. Select **14** (clicking on the **10** and typing **14** also works. This is especially useful when a size is not displayed in the list).

i *If row height has not been manually changed then an increase in font size automatically increases row height to display the text correctly.*

7. Select cells **B2:J2** and change the font size to **11**.

8. The formatting on any cell can be copied to other cell(s) using the **Format Painter**. Click on cell **B2**, click the **Format Painter** button, `✒` in the **Clipboard** group, then click and drag the range **B3:K4**. On release of the mouse button the formats from cell **B2** are painted to the range **B3:K4**.

9. Check that the cells in the range **B3:K4** are **Times New Roman** font, size 11pt and **bold**.

i *To use the **Format Painter** repeatedly, double click when selecting it and when finished painting the formatting, press <**Esc**> to turn it off.*

10. Leave the workbook open for the next Driving Lesson.

i *These changes can be made using the **Format Cells** dialog box. Click the **Format Cells** dialog box launcher to the right of the **Font** group name.*

Driving Lesson 64 - Format Number

▣ Park and Read

Numbers can be displayed in various styles, with decimal places, including a £ sign, % signs, with or without a separator to indicate thousands, etc.

☞ Manoeuvres

1.   Use the workbook **Climate** and select the range **B5:K16**.

2.   Click the **Number Format** box, | General ▾ | and select **More Number Formats** from the options displayed.

3.   The **Format Cells** dialog box is displayed. Select **Number** from the **Category** list.

4.   Check that the number of **Decimal places** is set as **2**. Leaving the **Use 1000 Separator (,)** unchecked, this will display numbers <u>without</u> the comma separator for thousands.

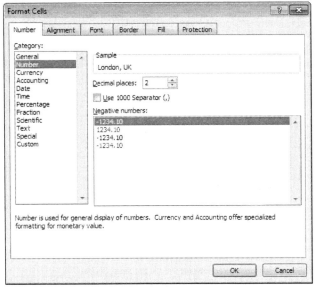

ℹ️   *In the **Negative numbers** section there are options to display any negative values in red, with or without a minus sign. Above this section is a check box **Use 1000 Separator (,)** which is used to add commas to numbers displaying thousands, e.g. **5,600**.*

5.   Click **OK** to apply the chosen formats. All the numbers in the range are now formatted with two decimal places <u>without</u> the thousands separator.

continued over

Driving Lesson 64 - Continued

6.   There are also buttons in the **Number** group to **Increase Decimal**, and **Decrease Decimal**, ![button], by one place for each click. With the cells **B5:K16** still selected, click the **Decrease Decimal** button, ![button]. The numbers are displayed with one decimal place.

> *After applying number formats, cells may display **########**. This means that the number is too big for the cell. The data is not lost but the column must be widened. This is covered in Driving Lesson 67.*

7.   Close the workbook <u>without</u> saving.

8.   Open the workbook **Budget**. This workbook contains cells with large numbers and currency values.

9.   Highlight the range **B7:N7**. To format this range as numbers with comma separators with no decimal places, display the **Format Cells** dialog box and from the **Number** tab, click **Number** in the **Category** list. Change the **Decimal places** to **0** and check **Use 1000 Separator (,)**. Click **OK**.

10. The tax rates are shown as decimals and would be better shown as percentages. Highlight the range **B12:M12**, display the **Format Cells** dialog box and from the **Number** tab, click **Percentage** in the **Category** list. Change the **Decimal places** to **0** and click **OK**.

11. The total rows are to be formatted as currency. Highlight the range **B4:N4**, and while holding down the **<Ctrl>** key, select the ranges **B10:N10** and **B14:N14**. The three separate ranges are now highlighted. Display the **Format Cells** dialog box and click **Currency** in the **Category** list. Change the **Decimal places** to **0**, add the **£** sign from the **Symbol** drop down list and under **Negative numbers** select to display negative numbers in red with a negative sign.

12. Click **OK**.

13. Format the ranges **B2:N2**, **B8:N9**, **B11:N11** and **B13:N13** as numbers, with no decimal places but with comma separators for thousands.

14. Print a **Landscape** copy of the worksheet, on a single sheet of **A4** paper.

15. Save the workbook as **Budget2** and close it.

Driving Lesson 65 - Dates

Park and Read

Date and **Time** are stored as numbers. The **Date** is a number representing the number of days since 1 January 1900. The **Time** is a decimal, as part of a day.

Both the **Date** and **Time** can be displayed in various formats including numbers and text.

Manoeuvres

1.   Start a new workbook.

2.   In cell **B2** enter your birthday, in the form of **24/2/88**. Press **<Enter>**.

3.   Make **B2** the active cell.

4.   Display the **Format Cells** dialog box, choose the **Number** tab.

5.   Select **Date** from the **Category** section and select each format from within **Type**. A preview is available in the **Sample** box.

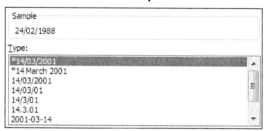

6.   Select **14 March 2001** format. Click **OK**.

*Selections within **Regional Settings** within the **Control Panel** affect the display of the date.*

7.   Click in cell **B4** and enter today's date by pressing **<Ctrl ;>**. This is the quick key press for the current date, it is entered as text. Press **<Enter>** to complete the entry.

8.   Repeat the above steps to display today's date in a different format.

9.   Click in cell **B6** and enter the current time by pressing **<Ctrl Shift ;>** Press **<Enter>**.

10.   Click in cell **B6**. To change the format of the time display the **Format Cells** dialog box, the **Number** tab is selected. Under **Time** all the **Types** include seconds. Select the **Category** as **Custom** and select with the **Type** as **h:mm AM/PM**. Click **OK**.

11.   Close the workbook <u>without</u> saving.

Driving Lesson 66 - Alignment

▣ Park and Read

Alignment is the positioning of text in a cell relative to its edges. By default **Labels** (text) are aligned to the left and **Numbers** to the right.

⌐ Manoeuvres

1. Open the workbook **House**.

2. Select the range **B3:N3**. To horizontally align these titles differently there are 3 buttons on the **Home** tab **Alignment** group: **Align Text Left**, ▤ (the default setting), **Center**, ▤ and **Align Text Right**, ▤.

3. Click the **Center** button, ▤, the labels are centred. Click the **Align Text Right** button, ▤, the labels are moved to the right.

4. Click on cell **A1**. There are also buttons for vertical alignment. They are **Top Align**, ▤, **Middle Align**, ▤, and **Bottom Align**, ▤ (the default setting). Click the **Middle Align** button. The text is in the centre of the cell, vertically.

5. The title is in cell **A1**. To centre it across the width of the worksheet, highlight the range **A1:N1** and click the **Merge & Center** button, ▤▾, in the **Alignment** group. The cells are merged, with the title in the centre.

6. The **Merge & Center** button has a drop down for other options. With the merged cell selected, click the **Merge & Center** drop down.

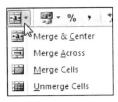

7. The options are displayed. This controls how the cells are merged. Click away from the menu without making a selection.

ⓘ *Cells already merged can be unmerged by clicking the button without using the drop down list.*

8. Rename the sheet as **House Finance**.

9. Insert a new worksheet.

continued over

Driving Lesson 66 - Continued

10. On the new **Sheet1**, create the following (note that the text **Telephone Extension** is all entered in cell **B3**, it flows into **C3**):

	A	B	C	D
1				
2				
3	Names	Telephone Extension		
4	John	356		
5	Asif	871		
6	Suzanne	780		
7	Mary	247		
8	Hardeep	163		
9				

11. Select the range **A3:B8** and change the **Font Size** to **9pt**.

12. When the label across the top of a column is too long for the information below, the text can be wrapped within the cell. Click on cell **B3** and click the **Wrap Text** button, ⊞, in the **Alignment** group.

 Text wrap can be applied to a range of cells - just select the range first.

13. The text in **B3** is wrapped within the cell and row height is increased automatically. Column **C** can now be used normally.

	A	B	C
1			
2			
3	Names	Telephone Extension	
4	John	356	
5	Asif	871	
6	Suzanne	780	
7	Mary	247	
8	Hardeep	163	
9			

The row height is only adjusted automatically if it has not been adjusted manually. Row height and column width are covered in the next lessons.

14. Save the workbook as **House2** and then close it.

Driving Lesson 67 - Changing Column Width

▣ Park and Read

Column Width is the distance across a column. It is measured in units. The size is **8.43** units - do not worry, as column widths are changed by dragging - if it looks right, then it is right.

↱ Manoeuvres

1. Open the workbook **Growth**. Enter your full name in **A1** and your age in **B1**.

2. Your name has probably been chopped off because it extends beyond the cell boundary. Your age is in cell **B1**. Column **A** needs to be widened.

3. Position the cursor in the **Column Border**, at the join between two columns, **A** and **B**. The mouse pointer changes to ✛.

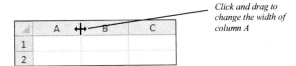

Click and drag to change the width of column A

4. Clicking and dragging to the left or right alters the width of the column to the left of the pointer (take care when dragging left, as a width of **0** results in the column being hidden). As the pointer moves, the current column width measurement is displayed next to the cursor, in units and pixels. Drag to the right to widen column **A** until your name is displayed fully.

5. Click the **Undo** button. To widen a column to fit to the largest entry, place the cursor between **A** and **B** in the column heading as before and **double click**. The column on the left is automatically adjusted to the widest entry in that column.

6. The longest cell entry is **POPULATION GROWTH (Millions)**, cell **A3**. Reduce the size of column **A** so that it only fits the width of your name.

7. More than one column can be adjusted at the same time. To adjust several columns, click and drag across the letters in the **Column Border**. Click on **C** and drag across to **D** to select two columns, release the mouse. Adjust either **C** or **D** to a width of **12** units.

8. Leave the workbook open for the next Driving Lesson.

ⓘ *There is also a menu option to change **Column Width**. Click the **Format** button in the **Cells** group and select **Column Width**. A number is then entered into the dialog box. Click **OK** to adjust the width.*

Driving Lesson 68 - Changing Row Height

█ Park and Read

Row Heights are increased to create more space between rows of data, making it easier to read the worksheet, or decreased to fit more data on a page.

Row heights are changed in the same way as changing column widths, except the adjust cursor is between two rows and it is the row above that is altered.

Manoeuvres

1. Using the workbook **Growth**, point in the **Row Border**, at the division between rows **4** and **5**. The mouse pointer changes to ✛.

2. The height of each row is **12.75** units. Clicking and dragging up or down now alters the height of the row above (take care when dragging up as a row can be hidden - **0** height). Carefully drag down to make the height of row **4** about **20**.

3. Select rows **5** to **12** by dragging in the **Row Border**. Adjust any row by dragging the adjust cursor down until **Height 18.00 (24 pixels)** is displayed.

4. Click on any cell to deselect the rows.

5. Place the cursor between the **6** and **7** in the row border, to display the adjust cursor.

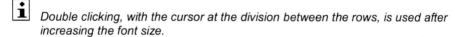

5	Asia	478	495
6	Africa	323	448
7	North America	212	265
8	South America	254	289
9	Europe	424	642

6. Double clicking the adjust cursor between the rows automatically adjusts the row above to the highest entry on that row. Double click and the row height is adjusted to the height of the text on row 6.

> ℹ️ *Double clicking, with the cursor at the division between the rows, is used after increasing the font size.*

7. Click the **Undo** button to return row **6** to its previous height.

8. Leave the workbook open for the next Driving Lesson.

> ℹ️ *There is also a menu option to change **Row Height**. Click the **Format** button in the **Cells** group and select **Row Height**. A specific height can then be entered into the dialog box. Click **OK** to apply the new height setting.*

Driving Lesson 69 - Inserting Rows and Columns

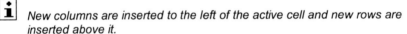 Park and Read

Rows and columns can be inserted into a worksheet between existing rows and columns when items have been forgotten or when new data is to be added.

A problem arises if a worksheet is fully developed with formulas in place. Rows or columns inserted at either end of a range, i.e. the first or last items, will mean an adjustment of all the formulas. **Check all formulas after inserting rows or columns**.

Manoeuvres

1. Using the workbook **Growth**, to insert a column between 1975 and 1990 (columns **C** and **D**), click on any cell in column **D**. On the **Home** tab, click the **Insert** drop down in the **Cells** group and select **Insert Sheet Columns**. A new column is inserted to the left of column **D**.

i *New columns are inserted to the left of the active cell and new rows are inserted above it.*

2. Click **Undo** to reverse the action. A column can be inserted using another method. Right click the column heading **D** and select **Insert** from the shortcut menu. A column is inserted.

3. Click **Undo** to reverse the action. Right click on any cell in column **D**. Select **Insert** and because the column was not selected *Excel* displays the **Insert** dialog box.

4. Select the **Entire column** option.

5. Click **OK**. A column is inserted. Rows are inserted in the same way.

6. Multiple rows and columns can be inserted by selecting the required number of rows or columns first. To insert 2 rows, click and drag the row numbers **4** and **5** and click the **Insert** button, in the **Cells** group. Two new rows are inserted as 4 and 5 above the selected rows.

7. Leave the workbook open for the next Driving Lesson.

Driving Lesson 70 - Deleting Rows and Columns

Park and Read

Unwanted extra rows or columns can be deleted.

Manoeuvres

1.   Use the workbook **Growth**.

2.   **Column B** is blank, except for your age and can be removed. Select column **B** by clicking in the column heading.

3.   Click **Delete** in the **Cells** group. Column **B** is now deleted and replaced by others moving across to the left.

4.   To delete rows **4** and **5**, select the two rows, right click and select **Delete**. Rows 4 and 5 are deleted and the other rows move up to fill the space.

5.   To remove row 2 by another method, right click in any cell on the row and select **Delete**.

6.   Select the required option in the **Delete** dialog box, in this case, **Entire row**. Click on **OK** to delete the row.

7.   Close the workbook <u>without</u> saving.

| i | *The results in cell formulas may be altered by deleting parts of the worksheet, resulting in errors, indicated by **#REF** in the cells.* |

Driving Lesson 71 - Adding Borders

▣ Park and Read

Borders are lines around the edges of cells. Border options are available to change the line style, colour and placement of border lines.

↱ Manoeuvres

1. Open the workbook **Rainfall**. One line has already been added under row 1. This line needs to be thicker.

2. Click cell **A1** and click the drop down arrow next to the **Borders** button, ▦▾, in the **Font** group to display the drop down list.

3. There are 13 border options and 5 drawing options, plus a **More Borders** button. Select the **Thick Bottom Border**. A thick line is added under the selected cell. Click away from the cell to see the results.

                                                                  continued over

Driving Lesson 71 - Continued

4. The last chosen option is displayed for future use on the **Borders** button. Highlight the range **B1:E1** and click the **Borders** <u>button</u> to apply the last chosen option, i.e. a thick bottom line.

5. More options are available using the **More Borders** option at the bottom of the menu. Highlight the range **A1:E13**, click the **Borders** drop down and select **More Borders** to display the **Border** tab in the **Format Cells** dialog box.

6. The grey line across the preview shows that there is a line in the selected range, but not on every cell.

7. Click twice on the centre line of the preview to remove it. If you have a problem click the **None** button in the **Presets**.

8. Lines are added to the range of selected cells by clicking the **Presets**, the **Border** buttons or the **Preview** diagram. To add a double line around the outside of the selected cells, click the last option under **Style**, the double line and then click the **Outline** button under **Presets**.

9. If coloured lines are required, the colour must be selected before adding the lines. To add gridline strength blue lines to the inside of the selected area, click the **Color** drop down and select **blue**.

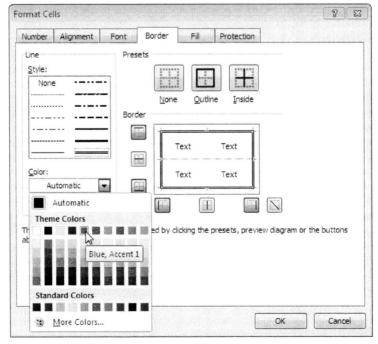

continued over

Driving Lesson 71 - Continued

10.   Then select the dotted line style option within the **Line Style** box and then click **Inside**. The **Preview** should look like below.

Text	Text
Text	Text

11.   Click **OK** to add the lines.

12.   When adding your own lines the gridlines on the worksheet can normally be turned off. Display the **Page Layout** tab and in the **Sheet Options** group, uncheck **View** under **Gridlines**.

13.   Add a thin line to all the cells in the range **A1:E1** (All Borders) using the **Border** button.

 *The **Format Painter**, ✎, can be used for copying borders as well as text, alignment and colour to other cells.*

14.   Print a copy of the worksheet.

15.   Close the workbook <u>without</u> saving.

Driving Lesson 72 - Adding Colour

🅿 Park and Read

Changing the colour of the text is similar to adding bold or italic - it highlights the text and it often looks better. *Excel* calls text colour, **Font Color**.

Manoeuvres

1. Open the workbook **Format**.

2. On the **Format** sheet, select the range **A2:A16**. Click the **Font Color** button, 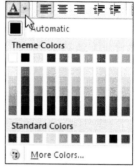. Click away from the range to see that it has changed to the colour shown on the **Font Color** button (**Red** is the default).

3. Select the same range, **A2:A16** and click the **Font Color** drop down, to display the colour box.

4. Select any **Blue** colour. Selecting a colour automatically closes the drop down box and adds that colour to the text in the selected range.

ℹ️ *The **Font Color** can also be changed using the **Format Cells** dialog box, **Font** tab, **Color** box, but it takes longer.*

5. Highlight the range **A16:N16** and change the text to **dark green**. Format the text in this range as **Bold**.

ℹ️ *The last colour used will be displayed on the button. **Red** is displayed as the text colour if the program is restarted.*

6. As well as changing the colour of the text, the cell background can be coloured. Highlight the range **A16:N16** and click the **Fill Color** button, drop down. Click on the lightest shade of **Olive Green**, to add the background colour.

7. Fill cell **A1** with a yellow shade and format the text as **Italic**. To copy the formatting from this cell, click **Format Painter**, .

8. Click on cell **A16** and notice how the format changes to match that in **A1**.

9. To make the range **B1:N1** look the same as **B16:N16**, select any cell in the range **B16:N16**, then click and click and drag over **B1:N1**.

10. Only if a colour printer is attached, print a copy of the worksheet.

11. Close the workbook <u>without</u> saving.

Driving Lesson 73 - Rotate Text

🅿 Park and Read

Text can be displayed vertically or at any angle within a cell.

👉 Manoeuvres

1.   Start a new workbook.

2.   In cell **A2** enter **Candidate** and your full name into cell **B2**.

3.   Click on cell **B2** and on the **Home** tab, click the **Orientation** button,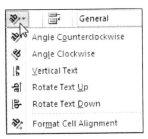
      in the **Alignment** group.

4.   Select **Vertical Text**. Your name is vertical and the row is increased in
      height automatically to hold the text.

ℹ️ *If the height of the row had been changed manually previously, then the row
height will not change automatically. Adjust the row height manually.*

5.   Click the **Undo** button, 🔄 to return the text to normal.

6.   To display text at angles not displayed on the menu,
      display the **Alignment** tab in the **Format Cells** dialog
      box by clicking the dialog box launcher in the
      Alignment group. Use the **Rotation** box on the right
      to drag the red diamond up to **45** degrees.

7.   Click **OK**.

8.   Repeat the last step but drag up to **90** degrees. Click
      OK. Double click the column heading border between
      B and **C** to reduce the width of column to fit the entry.
      This could be used to create a candidate register or for a form to log
      assignment results.

9.   Close the workbook <u>without</u> saving.

Driving Lesson 74 - Freezing Panes

🅿 Park and Read

Freeze Panes is used to keep some rows and/or columns in view all the time. This is generally used for labels, while scrolling through a large worksheet. Placement of the active cell is important before freezing as all rows above, and all columns to the left, are frozen.

🅿 Manoeuvres

1. Open the workbook **Accounts**. This shows the cash flow for a small hotel.

2. Before freezing the panes, one question: how much did the hotel pay in **October** for **Wages/NI** (National Insurance)?

3. Scrolling to the right loses columns at the left and, scrolling down, rows from the top. These important rows/columns on the screen can be frozen. Press <**Ctrl Home**> to return to cell **A1**, then click in cell **B4** (the first cell containing data).

4. Display the **View** tab and click **Freeze Panes** in the **Window** group. Select **Freeze Panes** from the menu. This freezes column **A** and rows **1** to **3**. Find **October's Wages/NI**, by scrolling down and across.

	A	I	J	K	L	M	N
1	Accounts for Year Er						
2							
3	Income	August	September	October	November	December	TOTAL
22	Rates	£0	£0	£0	£0	£0	£2,410
23	Electricity	£1,663	£0	£0	£1,205	£0	£6,510
24	Wages / NI	£6,042	£5,253	£4,276	£4,276	£5,463	£60,152
25	Insurance	£0	£0	£0	£0	£0	£3,970
26	Administration	£548	£553	£429	£372	£501	£5,872
27	Advertising	£800	£400	£400	£650	£700	£8,050
28	Spending	£16,779	£15,209	£11,510	£14,287	£19,035	£189,656

 If panes are frozen when a worksheet is saved, they will be still be frozen when the workbook is re-opened.

5. When removing the frozen panes, the placing of the active cell is not important. Click the **Freeze Panes** button and then **Unfreeze Panes**.

6. Click on cell **A4** and select **Freeze Panes**. This freezes rows 1, 2 and 3 only. Scroll around the worksheet to see the effect.

7. Remove the frozen panes with **Unfreeze Panes**.

8. Select **Freeze Panes** and then choose **Freeze First Column**. This freezes column **A** only. Scroll around the worksheet to see the effect.

9. Select **Unfreeze Panes** to remove the frozen panes, then close the workbook <u>without</u> saving.

Driving Lesson 75 - Zoom

P Park and Read

Zoom is used to control the magnification of the worksheet window to see more by making the worksheet smaller, or to see less by making it bigger. The **Zoom** percentage is saved with the worksheet. **Zoom** is purely visual and does not affect the printing of the worksheet.

This Driving Lesson is affected by the screen resolution. This was prepared on a screen with a 1024x768 resolution. More or less of the worksheet may be seen.

Manoeuvres

1. Open the workbook **Shop**. This is a worksheet to show the profitability of a small market stall, selling one item.

2. The **Zoom** slider is located at the right end of the **Status Bar**.

3. This is used by either dragging the slider left to decrease the percentage (to see more), or the right to increase the percentage. The buttons at either end can also be used to make bigger changes. Click and drag the slider to the left to display **80%**. The worksheet window is resized to **80%**.

4. Use to increase the percentage to **120%**.

5. Experiment with the **Zoom** slider.

6. There is a **Selection** option that fits a worksheet in the visible window. The required range must be selected first. Highlight the range **A1:N1** (the whole width of the worksheet).

7. In the **View** tab, the **Zoom** group, click the **Zoom to Selection** button. The screen fits the selection.

8. Click the **Zoom** button, ⌕ Zoom

9. Any percentage can be set exactly by typing directly into the **Custom** box, within the **Zoom** dialog box. Enter **118** and press <**Enter**> or click **OK**.

10. Close the workbook <u>without</u> saving.

Driving Lesson 76 - Revision

This Driving Lesson covers the features introduced in this section. Try not to refer to the preceding Driving Lessons while completing it.

1. Open the workbook **Balance Sheet**.

2. The **Balance Sheet 2008** is displayed. To add a centred title, insert two rows at the top of the sheet.

3. Add the title **Balance Sheet 2008** in **A1**. Change to font size of the title to **16pt** and the merge and centre from **A** to **O**.

4. Add **Freeze Panes** to keep **Rows 1** to **3** and **Columns A & B** on the screen permanently.

5. Scroll to see the effect of the freeze.

6. What was the **Shareholders Equity** for **Aug**?

7. Remove the **Freeze Panes**.

8. Using the zoom control display the information to fit within the screen.

9. Change the **Zoom** back to **100%**.

10. Which year has been the most profitable?

11. Change the orientation of the page to **Landscape** and preview the worksheet.

12. Change the print options to fit the worksheet to one piece of paper.

13. Print one copy of **Balance Sheet 2008**.

14. Close the workbook <u>without</u> saving the changes.

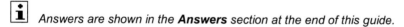 *Answers are shown in the **Answers** section at the end of this guide.*

If you experienced any difficulty completing this Revision refer back to the Driving Lessons in this section. Then redo the Revision.

Driving Lesson 77 - Revision

This Driving Lesson covers the features introduced in this section. Try not to refer to the preceding Driving Lessons while completing it.

1.   Open the workbook **Apples**.

2.   Change the contents of cell **A1** to font size **16pt**.

3.   Right align the labels at the top of the columns, including **Total**, i.e. the range **B3:E3**.

4.   Change the **Zoom** percentage to **125**.

5.   Change the display format for the numbers in the range **B8:E11** to currency with no decimal places, with negative numbers shown in red with no symbol.

6.   Change the width of **Column A** to **12.00** units

7.   Widen columns **B** to **E** to **10.00** units.

8.   Increase the row height of **Row 3** to **19.50** units.

9.   Increase to height of rows **4** to **11** to **15.00** units.

10.   Change the vertical alignment of the range **A3:E3** to the centre of the cells.

11.   Insert a new column **D** to add **Grapes** to the worksheet. Add the title, **Grapes**. The numbers sold are 0, 1 and 5.

12.   Complete the formula to total the new column in **D7**.

13.   **Grapes** are bought at **£8** and sold at **£15**. Add this data and the appropriate formulas to cell **D9** and **D11**. What is the **Total Profit** now?

14.   Add lines to the inside of the range **A3:F11** and a double line to the outside and remove the gridlines from the screen.

15.   Change the colour of the labels to **Blue** and the background colour (**Fill Color** button) to the range **A3:F11** to **Light Orange**.

16.   Print a copy of the worksheet.

17.   Save the workbook as **Apples2** and close it.

If you experienced any difficulty completing this Revision refer back to the Driving Lessons in this section. Then redo the Revision.

Once you are confident with the features, complete the Record of Achievement Matrix referring to the section at the end of the guide. Only when competent move on to the next Section.

Section 9
Functions &
Addressing

By the end of this Section you should be able to:

Use Paste Function

Use the Functions Sum, Count & Average

Use the Functions Max, Min and IF

Use Relative and Absolute Addressing

To gain an understanding of the above features, work through the **Driving Lessons** in this **Section**.

For each **Driving Lesson**, read the **Park and Read** instructions, without touching the keyboard, then work through the numbered steps of the **Manoeuvres** on the computer. Complete the **Revision Exercise(s)** at the end of the section to test your knowledge.

Driving Lesson 78 - Functions

▣ Park and Read

Functions are specialised formulas that make a calculation easier. Just as **Sum** totals a range of cells, other functions such as **Average**, **Min**, **Max** and **Count** can be used to simplify calculations.

Functions can be typed directly into a cell, e.g. **=SUM(A1:B6)** or **Insert Function** can be used to insert the formula structure e.g. **=SUM()**, prior to selecting a range of cells to complete the formula.

☞ Manoeuvres

1. On a new worksheet, enter a column of 10 numbers, starting in **B3**.

2. Click cell **B13**. To add the numbers type **=s** the list functions starting with **s** is displayed, scroll the list and double click **SUM**. Type the rest of the function **B3:B12)** and press **<Enter>** to complete the formula.

3. Enter numbers into the cells **D2**, **D3**, **D4** and **D5**.

4. Click cell **D7**, then click the **Insert Function** button, f_x, on the **Formula Bar** to display the **Insert Function** dialog box.

5. Click on each **Category** in the drop down list of the **Or select a category** to see all available functions.

6. Select the **Math & Trig** category and from **Select a function**, scroll down the list and select **Sum**. An explanation of the function is given.

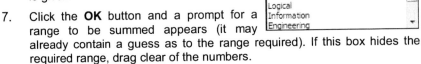

7. Click the **OK** button and a prompt for a range to be summed appears (it may already contain a guess as to the range required). If this box hides the required range, drag clear of the numbers.

8. Click the **Collapse** button, 🔽, at the right side of the **Number1** box. Click and drag to select the range **D2:D5**. Click the **Expand** button, 🔼, in the box.

9. Click **OK**. The function is entered into the worksheet and the result is displayed.

10. Close the worksheet <u>without</u> saving.

Driving Lesson 79 - Count

🅿 Park and Read

The function **COUNT** counts the cells that contain numbers in a range. **COUNTA** counts the number of cells that are <u>not</u> empty and **COUNTBLANK** counts empty cells in a range.

↱ Manoeuvres

1. Open the workbook **Marks**. This shows the exam results for one pupil, **Ali Kazan**. The task is to add the calculations, in the form of functions, to rate the candidate's performance.

2. Click on cell **E7** and click the **Insert Function** button, *fx*.

3. Click on **Statistical** in the **Select a category** list and then select **COUNT** in the **Select a function** list.

4. Click **OK** to display the **Function Arguments** box. Move the dialog box, if necessary, to see the cells.

5. Select the range **B4:B21** (the cells that might contain numbers).

 COUNT works only on cells that contain numbers; *COUNTA* works when applied to cells including numbers and/or text. Both count zeros but not empty cells.

6. Click **OK** to complete the function.

7. **Ali** failed to turn up for the German exam. Enter **0** in cell **B8**. The number of subjects now shows one more as **Zero** counts as a number.

8. Delete the function in cell **E7**.

9. Click **Insert Function**, *fx*, again and this time select **COUNTBLANK** from **Statistical**.

10. Select the range **B4:B21** and click **OK**.

11. Notice how the number of blank cells has been counted.

12. Delete this function and replace it with the original **COUNT** function.

13. Leave the workbook open for the next Driving Lesson.

Driving Lesson 80 - Average & Round

🅿 Park and Read

Average adds a list of numbers and divides by the number of numbers.

Sometimes it is required to show numerical data to a specific level of precision, for example to show a price field to the nearest pound or an age to the nearest year. To do this: either use formatting (which does not change the actual content) or use the **Round** function.

↱ Manoeuvres

1. The workbook **Marks** should be open from the last exercise, if not open it.

2. Click in cell **E8**. Click the **Insert Function** button, 𝆑.

3. Click on **Statistical** in the **Function category** list and select **AVERAGE** in the **Select a function** list.

4. Click **OK** to display the **Function Arguments** box for **AVERAGE**. Drag it to the right of the screen, away from the marks.

5. Select the range **B4:B21** (the cells that might contain numbers, the box collapses and on release of the mouse expands again). Click **OK** to complete the function.

6. The **0** for **German** is reducing the average. It is decided that **Ali** should not have been registered for **German**, delete the zero in cell **B8**. Note the increase in **Average** mark.

7. With the workbook **Marks** open, start a new workbook. In cell **B3** enter **27.32** and in cell **B4** enter **27.68**.

8. Highlight **B3:B4** and format the range as **Number** with **0** decimal places. Click **OK**. The numbers are displayed to the nearest whole number. The cell content has not been changed, only the appearance. **B4** displays **28** in the cell. Click on **B4**. The **Formula Bar** still shows the cell content as **27.68**.

9. Undo the formatting and in **C3** enter the formula **=B3*1.15** to calculate the new value for **B3** after a 15% increase. Copy the formula down to **C4**.

10. In **D3** enter the formula **=ROUND(C3,0)**. This rounds the value in **C3** to have **0** decimal places. Copy the formula down to **D4**. The values are shown as whole numbers.

ℹ️ *The **Round** function could have been applied directly with the calculation as =ROUND((B3*1.15),0). This would calculate the new value and apply the rounding in one formula.*

11. Close the workbook <u>without</u> saving, but leave the workbook **Marks** open.

Driving Lesson 81 - Maximum and Minimum

P Park and Read

MAX   the function for maximum, finds and displays the largest number in the
          selected range.

MIN   the function for minimum, finds and displays the smallest number in the
          selected range.

Manoeuvres

1. The workbook **Marks** should still be open. If not, open it.

2. Enter the text **Highest Mark** in cell **D9** and **Lowest Mark** in cell **D10**.

3. Click in cell **E9**. Click the **Insert Function** button, f_x.

4. Click on **Statistical** in the **Function category** list and select **MAX** in the
    Select a function list.

5. Click **OK** to display the **MAX** box.

6. Select the same range as before **B4:B21**.

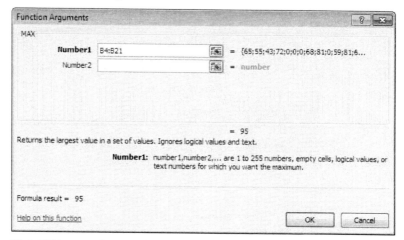

7. Click **OK** to complete the function. The highest mark is **95**.

8. In cell **E10** enter the **MIN** function using the same range to display the
    lowest mark.

9. To test the four functions created, change the marks in **B17** to **50** and **B6**
    to **83** and note the changes in the function values.

10. Save the workbook as **Marks2** and then close it.

Driving Lesson 82 - IF

▣ Park and Read

The logical function **IF** compares the contents of a cell and, if a logical test is met, performs one action; if not, it performs another.

=IF(Logical_test,Value_if_true,Value_if_false)

For instance, if the value in cell **A1** is greater than 10 then multiply it by 3, if not, multiply it by 2. This is expressed as: **=IF(A1>10,A1*3,A1*2)**

The **IF** function is sometimes described as **IF THEN ELSE**. **IF** the condition is true **THEN** do this **ELSE** do that. The parts are separated by commas.

↷ Manoeuvres

1.   On a blank worksheet, enter the labels **Interest Calculation** in **B1**, **Balance** in cell **B3** and **Interest** in cell **B4**.

2.   Enter **200** in **C3** for your bank balance.

3.   The interest on your money depends on whether the balance is over or under **£100**. Click in cell **C4** and as an alternative to using the **Insert Function** button, display the **Formulas** tab and click **Logical** in the **Function Library**. Select **IF** from the list.

4.   Enter the following parts of the test with a mixture of pointing at cell references and typing.

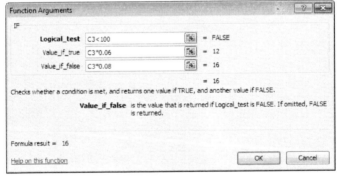

5.   Click **OK** to complete the function. The function looks at the value of cell **C3** and if it is less than **100**, calculates the interest at **6%** of the value, otherwise it calculates it at **8%**.

6.   The result of the function, the interest, depends on the balance. Move to **C3** and enter **1000**. The interest is **£80**, the higher rate (8%). Enter **50** and the interest is **£3** (6%). Experiment, change the balance and see the interest change. The **IF** function is very powerful.

7.   Close the workbook <u>without</u> saving.

Driving Lesson 83 - Relative Addressing

▣ Park and Read

As a formula is copied to a new location, by default the cell references in the formula change automatically. The new calculation is performed on cells in the same positions relative to the original formula, e.g. references to **B2+B3** become **C2+C3** then **D2+D3**, as the formula is copied to the right from column to column. This is Relative Addressing.

↷ Manoeuvres

1.   Start a new workbook.

2.   In **B2** enter **7** and **B3** enter **8**.

3.   Select cell **B4** and click the **AutoSum** button, on the **Formulas** tab, **Function Library** group, to add the contents of the two cells above. Press <**Enter**> to accept the range and perform the calculation. The answer should be **15** and the formula **=SUM(B2:B3)**.

4.   Use the **Fill Handle** to copy this formula across to cell **C4**. The displayed answer is **0** because the two cells above are empty. Click on cell **C4** to display the formula, it is **=SUM(C2:C3)**. It sums the two cells directly above.

5.   Enter **3** in cell **C2** and **5** in cell **C3**. The answer in cell **C4** is **8**.

6.   Copy cell **B4** to cell **E8**. What is the formula in cell **E8**?

7.   Enter any two numbers in the cells **E6** and **E7** to test the formula.

8.   Close the workbook <u>without</u> saving.

9.   Open the workbook **Accounts**. This is the basic cash flow (the flow of money in and out) for a small hotel.

10.   Click on cell **B14**. This sums the cash coming into the hotel for **January** (**Turnover**).

11.   Use any method to copy this formula to the range **C14:N14**.

12.   Click on cell **E14** (the turnover for **April**). It sums the same range of rows as in cell **B14**, except using the cells in column **E**.

13.   Close the workbook <u>without</u> saving.

🛈 *The answer is shown in the **Answers** section at the end of this guide.*

Driving Lesson 84 - Absolute Addressing

P Park and Read

Absolute addressing is used when the same cell is to be used even when copying formulas. When formulas use the same cell, it is easy to make changes to all the formulas.

The **Absolute** reference key is the **$** sign. **D7** is a **Relative** address that will change if the formula is copied and **$D$7** is an **Absolute** address that will stay the same. The dollar signs fix the cell so that it copies without changing.

Manoeuvres

1. Open the workbook **World Population**. This workbook contains some population statistics.

2. The population of Europe in 1975 was **424** million. The world population was **1953** million. Click on cell **C8**, Europe's population as a percentage of the world. Note the formula **=B8/$B$11**. The cell **B11** has been made **Absolute** and does not change in the formulas in column **C**.

3. Close the workbook <u>without</u> saving.

4. Open the workbook **Absolute**.

5. The average mark is calculated in cell **B23** as **63**. Click in cell **B23** and view the formula (the **Average** function).

6. To compare each mark with the average, click in cell **C4** and enter the formula **=B4-B23** using any method. The answer is **2** (65 is 2 marks above the average of 63).

7. If the formula is left as **Relative**, the other cells will not work. Copy the formula in cell **C4** to cell **C5**. The formula is **=B5-B24** the cells have moved down one row. **B24** is empty, therefore the answer is **55**.

8. Delete the contents of cell **C5**. Click in cell **C4**. The cell reference **B23** needs to be fixed, i.e. made **Absolute**. Change **B23** to **$B$23**.

9. Use the **Fill Handle** or any other method to copy cell **C4** down the range **C5:C21**. The average mark **63** is used in all the formulas in column **C**.

10. Change the **English Literature** mark to **72**. All the cells in the range **C4:C21** have changed because **B23** has changed.

11. Close the workbook <u>without</u> saving.

Driving Lesson 85 - Revision

This Driving Lesson covers the features introduced in this section. Try not to refer to the preceding Driving Lessons while completing it.

1. What name is given to cell references in a formula which change when the formula is copied to a new location?

2. What symbol is used to show that references are **Absolute**?

3. If a formula in a cell is **=C2+$E$5** what would the formula be if this was copied a) down one cell? b) to the right one cell?

4. If you copied the formula **=B3+D4** in **C6** to cell **F8**, what would the formula be in cell **F8**? You can create this on a worksheet if it helps.

5. When would you use **Absolute Addressing**?

6. Start a new workbook and create the worksheet below.

◢	A	B	C	D	E
1					
2					
3		Number Sold		20	
4		Buying Price		5	
5		Selling Price		6	
6		Profit			
7					

7. The reason for using column **D** for the numbers is that the text is too long for column **B**. It spilled over into column **C**. Widen column **B** to hold all the text.

8. Delete column **C**.

9. Calculate the **Profit** in **C6** (remember brackets).

10. Change the **Number Sold** to **534**, the **Buying Price** to **2.56** and the **Selling Price** to **3.99**.

11. Format cell **C6** to display currency with two decimal places.

12. How much is the **Profit**?

13. Close the workbook <u>without</u> saving.

i   *Answers are shown in the **Answers** section at the end of this guide.*

If you experienced any difficulty completing this Revision refer back to the Driving Lessons in this section. Then redo the Revision.

Driving Lesson 86 - Revision

This Driving Lesson covers the features introduced in this section. Try not to refer to the preceding Driving Lessons while completing it.

1. The following data represents sales figures for a group of salespersons. Construct the spreadsheet and add the data at the positions shown.

	A	B	C	D
1	Analysis of Sales Figures			
2				
3	Salesperson	Sales	Average +/-	
4	Smith	1300		
5	Brown	8965		
6	Bloggs	21050		
7	White	17800		
8	Green			
9	Chapman	670		
10	Hall	1809		
11				
12	Total			
13	Average Sales			
14	No of Salespersons			
15	Lowest Sales			
16	Highest Sales			
17				

2. Enter the functions for **Total** and **Average Sales** in **B12** and **B13**.

3. The number of salespersons is calculated using the **COUNT** function (Remember to count the sales figures, not the salespersons' names).

4. The high and low sales use **MAX** and **MIN**. Similar to **Count** but display the largest and smallest. They can be found in **Statistical** listed under **More Functions**.

5. The **Average +/-** column is to be the variation of an individual's sales compared to the average, calculated by subtracting the average sales value from the individual's sales. For **C4** this is **=B4-B13** (Remember **Absolute** and **Relative** addressing if copying formulas down the column).

6. Print a copy of the worksheet.

7. Save the workbook as **Sales** then close it.

i It is very important to decide whether to put a zero in cell **B8** or to leave it blank. Try it! The answers will be different.

If you experienced any difficulty completing this Revision refer back to the Driving Lessons in this section. Then redo the Revision.

Once you are confident with the features, complete the Record of Achievement Matrix referring to the section at the end of the guide. Only when competent move on to the next Section.

Section 10
Charts

By the end of this Section you should be able to:

Create a Chart

Select Chart Type

Move, Copy and Resize Charts

Format a Chart

Print Charts

Use Chart Options

To gain an understanding of the above features, work through the **Driving Lessons** in this **Section**.

For each **Driving Lesson**, read the **Park and Read** instructions, without touching the keyboard, then work through the numbered steps of the **Manoeuvres** on the computer. Complete the **Revision Exercise(s)** at the end of the section to test your knowledge.

Driving Lesson 87 - Introducing Charts

🅿 Park and Read

It can be difficult to find vital information like changes in trends or performance from rows and columns of numeric data. A picture of the figures, **a graph or chart**, helps to identify subtle changes that may have otherwise been missed. Some of the standard chart types available are:

Column	-	Shaded vertical columns
Bar	-	Shaded horizontal bars
Line	-	Points connected by a line
Pie	-	Data as slices of a circular pie

There are also various 3-D versions and different versions of the same chart type.

There are two ways in which charts can be created: as part of a worksheet, appearing on the sheet, with the data (an **Embedded** chart) or as a completely separate sheet, **Chart1**.

Manoeuvres

1. Open the workbook **Charts**. This workbook contains both an embedded chart and charts created on separate sheets.

2. Click the **London Rainfall** sheet. This is a chart that has been created on a separate sheet.

3. Click the **Data** sheet. This sheet contains the source information used for the charts. Scroll down the worksheet to see the embedded chart under the data.

4. Click the **Mumbai Rainfall** sheet. This is a chart similar to the **London Rainfall** on a separate sheet.

5. Close the workbook **Charts** <u>without</u> saving.

Driving Lesson 88 - Creating Charts

 Park and Read

Created charts are, by default, placed on the same sheet as the data. This is called an **Embedded Chart**. Embedded charts can be moved, resized or deleted.

Manoeuvres

1. Open the workbook **Rainfall**. This workbook contains the average rainfall for four major cities in the world. Charts are to be created to show this information.

2. To chart **London's** rainfall, as a column chart, select the range **A1:B13** (this is the rainfall and the labels).

3. Display the **Insert** tab and click the **Column** button in the **Charts** group.

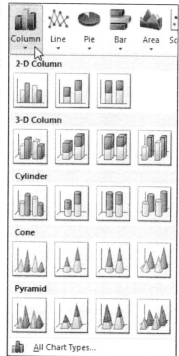

4. The **Column** chart options are displayed. Under **2-D Column** select the first option **Clustered Column**. The chart is embedded and placed on the **Rainfall** sheet with the data.

5. The chart is active and the **Ribbon** displays a new group of tabs under the banner **Chart Tools**. The **Design** tab is selected.

6. The chart can be moved by clicking and dragging. Place the cursor on the chart border (it displays a four-headed arrow). click and drag it to the left and below the data.

7. To resize the chart, click and drag on any of the handles around it (any corner or the centre of any side), inwards will make it smaller or outwards to make it larger. The cursor changes to a double-headed arrow. Click the centre on the right edge and drag to the right about the width of another column to make the chart wider. Any handle can be used to resize.

> To delete an embedded chart, click on it to select it and press the <**Delete**> key.

8. Save the workbook as **Rainfall2** and leave it open.

Driving Lesson 89 - Moving Charts Between Worksheets

 Park and Read

After the chart has been created it can be moved and placed on a separate worksheet.

 Manoeuvres

1.   The workbook **Rainfall2** should still be open, if not, open it. A column chart of the rainfall in **Mumbai** is going to be created.

2.   Two separate ranges need to be selected to chart **Mumbai's** rainfall, the labels and the actual rainfall data. Select **A1:A13** and hold <Ctrl> down while selecting the other range **C1:C13**.

	A	B	C	D	E	F
1	RAINFALL(cms)	London	Mumbai	Adelaide	Tokyo	
2	Jan	5.5	0.5	1.8	5.0	
3	Feb	4.0	0.5	1.8	7.0	
4	Mar	3.8	0.0	2.5	10.0	
5	Apr	3.9	0.0	4.0	14.0	
6	May	4.5	2.0	7.0	13.0	
7	Jun	4.5	24.0	8.0	18.0	
8	Jul	5.8	24.0	7.0	14.0	
9	Aug	6.0	24.0	6.0	14.0	
10	Sep	5.5	24.0	5.0	21.0	
11	Oct	6.0	4.5	4.5	22.0	
12	Nov	6.3	1.0	3.0	10.0	
13	Dec	4.3	0.0	2.5	6.0	
14						

3.   Display the **Insert** tab and click the **Column** button in the **Charts** group.

4.   The **Column** chart options are displayed as before. Select the same option, a **Clustered Column**. The chart is embedded and placed on the **Rainfall** sheet with the data, overlapping the data and the previous chart.

5.   The chart can be moved by clicking and dragging. You need to select the chart first; click on the **Chart Area**. Drag it to the right so that it doesn't overlap the data or the other embedded chart.

6.   To place the chart on a separate worksheet, click the **Move Chart** button on the **Design** tab. The **Move Chart** dialog box is displayed.

7.   Select the **New sheet** option and enter the sheet name **Mumbai Rainfall** as a replacement for **Chart1**.

continued over

Driving Lesson 89 - Continued

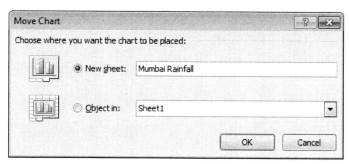

8. Click **OK** to move the chart.

9. The chart has a **Legend** (Legends show which columns belong to which data series) added and as there is only one set of data, it can be removed. Display the **Layout** tab. Click the **Legend** button and select **None**. The **Legend** is removed.

10. To add axis titles to the chart, click the **Axis Titles** button and select **Primary Horizontal Axis Title**. Select **Title Below Axis**, type **Months** and press **<Enter>**.

11. To add vertical axis title to the chart, click the **Axis Titles** button and select **Primary Vertical Axis Title**. Select **Rotated Title** and type **Rainfall (cm)** and press **<Enter>**.

12. Save the workbook using the same name **Rainfall2**.

13. Close the **Rainfall2** workbook.

Driving Lesson 90 - Chart Types

▣ Park and Read

Different types of chart are used for different data. The most common type of chart is a **Column** chart as seen already. It displays the data in columns and is used to compare values. **Bar** charts are column charts where the values are horizontal bars and not vertical columns. **Line** charts are used to display the movement of values as with sales or profits over time. **Pie** charts display the values as slices of circle. The size of each slice represents the value of the data on which it is based, as a fraction of the total. Pie charts are used to show values as a part of the whole as with product costs or expenditure.

⌐ Manoeuvres

1. Open the workbook **Computer Data**. Four different types of chart are to be created using the same data to show the different representations of each.

2. Highlight the data in the cells **A3:B8** (include the titles but not the totals, as they are rarely included in charts).

3. Display the **Insert** tab and from the **Charts** group, click **Pie**. Select the first option a basic **Pie**.

4. The **Chart title**, **Computer Sales** is added automatically.

5. Move the chart to a separate worksheet. Name the sheet, **Pie Chart**.

6. Return to the **Data** sheet and using the same range, create a basic **Column** chart on a new sheet named **Column Chart**.

7. Repeat the last step to create a **Bar Chart** and then again to create a **Line Chart**. The sheet tabs should be as in the diagram:

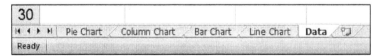

 *To change the chart type, first select the chart. From the **Chart Tools Design** tab, click the **Change Chart Type** button in the **Type** group and select an alternative.*

8. Leave the workbook open for the next Driving Lesson.

Driving Lesson 91 - Copy, Move & Resize Charts

🅿 Park and Read

Charts can be copied, resized and deleted.

↱ Manoeuvres

1.   The **Computer Data** workbook should still be open.

2.   Charts can be copied from one sheet to another. Click the **Bar Chart** sheet tab.

3.   Click the **Copy** button, or press <**Ctrl C**>.

4.   To copy the chart to the **Data** sheet, display it, select cell **A11** and then click the **Paste** button, or press <**Ctrl V**> to paste the chart on to the **Data** sheet.

5.   The chart is too big. Drag a corner handle towards the centre of the chart to reduce its size until the whole chart and the data fits on the screen.

6.   Charts can be copied from workbook to workbook. Copy the **Line Chart**.

7.   Start a new workbook. Paste the chart on to **Sheet1**.

8.   If the chart is required on a separate sheet and not embedded as it is now, display the **Design** tab, move the chart and name the sheet as **Line Chart** and click **OK**.

ℹ️ *Embedded charts are moved from book to book using **Cut**, ✂ or <**Ctrl X**> and*

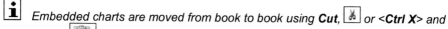

Paste, 📋 *, or <**Ctrl V**> the same method used for moving a range. Charts on separate sheets are moved from book to book using the same method as moving a normal worksheet, see Section 5.*

9.   Close the new workbook <u>without</u> saving.

10. Display the **Data** sheet of the **Computer Data** workbook.

11. Click on the embedded bar chart on the **Data** sheet to select it and then click **Copy**. Place the active cell beneath the chart and click **Paste** to create a duplicate.

12. To delete the original embedded chart, click the chart and then press <**Delete**>. The embedded chart is removed. Delete the other bar chart.

13. Save the workbook as **Computer Data2** and leave it open.

Driving Lesson 92 - Formatting Charts

▣ Park and Read

All parts of a chart, including the colours, axes, text, gridlines, chart and plot area, can be changed.

⌐ Manoeuvres

1. The workbook **Computer Data2** should still be open, if not open it.

2. Select the **Bar Chart** sheet tab. Place the mouse cursor on different parts of the chart and read the **ToolTips**.

3. Click the chart title **Computer Sales** and press <**Delete**> to remove it.

4. Any and every part of a chart can be changed by formatting. Point at the background (none by default), the **Plot Area** and click.

5. Display the **Format** tab. The **Shape Styles** group buttons can be used. Click **Shape Fill** and select a light orange colour.

ℹ️ *The **Gradient** and **Texture** options can be used from the same menu to vary a flat colour.*

ℹ️ *The colour of the background to a chart is more important if viewed on screen. Printed charts can be left as the default (no fill colour) to save ink or toner.*

6. Click the **Column Chart** sheet to make it active.

7. To change the colour of the columns, point at any column and then click to select them. Change the colour to **Red** using the **Shape Fill** button.

ℹ️ *Any part of a chart can be clicked to select it and then formatted. Only the options that can be changed will be available.*

8. The colour of a single data point can also be changed. To change the Sunderland column to blue, the correct column has to be selected. Click away from the columns. Click the **Sunderland** column (to select the entire series) and click again to select the single data point (circular handles are displayed around it).

9. Select **Blue** using the **Shape Fill** button.

10. Display the **Pie Chart** and using the same technique change the colour of the **Sunderland** slice to **Yellow** (under **Standard Colors**).

11. A feature specific to **Pie Charts** is the ability to explode all or a single slice. With the **Sunderland** slice selected, click and drag outwards slightly from the centre, release the mouse to drop the slice; this slice is now highlighted to draw attention to it.

12. Save the workbook using the same name and leave it open.

Driving Lesson 93 - Chart Options

▣ Park and Read

To make any changes to a chart, the chart or specific part of the chart has to be selected by clicking on the relevant part first. This displays the **Chart** tab from which controls all the **Chart Options**.

All parts of a chart, including the titles, legend, data labels and chart type can be changed. Text boxes can also be added to include supporting information.

⌐ Manoeuvres

1. The workbook **Computer Data2** should still be open, if not open it and display the **Pie Chart**.

2. Text can be added to charts via text boxes. Display the **Layout** tab and click the **Text Box** button in the **Insert** group.

3. Click and drag a rectangle in the centre of the **Sunderland** slice. On releasing the mouse the cursor is placed in the box, type **Sunderland** and click away from the box when complete. A text box is moved by dragging its border.

4. Click once on the text box, to select its contents (it will display a border). The text can now be changed and formatted. Increase the font size to **14** and make it *italic*. The size of the text box may need increasing. Click away from the box to deselect it.

5. To delete a text box, select it to enter edit mode, then click the border to display a solid border and press **<Delete>**. Delete the **Sunderland** text box from the **Pie Chart** in this way. Click away from the pie chart to deselect the **Sunderland** slice.

6. Data labels can be displayed on the chart. Display the **Layout** tab and click the **Data Labels** button in the **Labels** group.

7. Click **More Data Label Options** to display the **Format Data Labels** dialog box.

8. In the **Label Options** section, under **Label Contains** check the **Category Name** and **Value** options and under **Label Position** select the **Outside End** option, click **Close**.

9. Display the **Format Data Labels** dialog box again. In **Label Contains**, remove the **Category Name** and **Value** options and select **Percentage**. In **Label Position** select **Inside End** and click **Close**.

10. To remove the data labels, click the **Data Labels** button and select **None** or display the **Format Data Labels** dialog box and click to remove the checks from the options not required and click **Close**.

continued over

Driving Lesson 93 - Continued

i   *The **Labels** group also controls the **Chart Title**, **Axis Titles** and **Legend**.*

11. Display the **Bar Chart** sheet. Right click on the **Legend** and select **Format Legend**. Select **Fill** from the options on the left. Select **Solid Fill**, choose a pale colour from the **Color** drop down. Click **Close** and the legend is filled with colour.

12. Add a chart title of the type, **Centered Overlay Title** and edit the **Chart Title** to **Computer Sales 2009**.

13. Highlight the title text and right click to display a shortcut menu and some formatting options for the text. Change the font size to **28**, click the **Font Color** button and select a **Blue** from the colour palette. The size and colour of the title text is changed.

i   *The chart axes text and legend text are changed in the same way.*

14. Remove the legend by clicking the **Legend** button and selecting **None**.

15. The type of chart can be changed. With the **Bar Chart** still displayed, display the **Design** tab and click the **Change Chart Type** button.

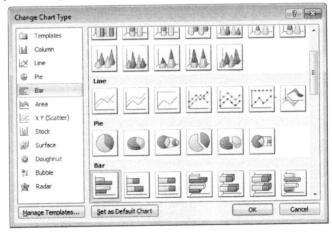

16. With **Bar** still selected as the main type, select **Clustered Bar in 3-D**. Click **OK**.

i   *Any chart can be changed in a similar way.*

17. Make the **Line Chart** active. To format the line, click on it to select it. Display the **Format** tab and click the **Shape Outline** button. From the menu select **Red** from the **Standard Colors** section.

18. Click the **Shape Outline** button again, click **Weight** and then select **3pt** as the thickness. The line is now red and thicker.

19. Save the workbook using the same name and leave it open.

Driving Lesson 94 - Printing Charts

🅿 Park and Read

Charts created on a new worksheet are printed as a normal worksheet, via the **File** tab and the **Print** option.

Embedded charts can be printed with the rest of the sheet using the commands already stated. An embedded chart can be printed by itself by selecting it before selecting the **Print** command.

Manoeuvres

1. The workbook **Computer Data2** should still be open. If not open it.

2. To print the **Column Chart**, display the correct sheet. Click the **File** tab and select **Print** or press <**Ctrl P**> then click the **Print** button. A single copy of the chart is printed using the default settings.

3. Click the **Data** sheet, highlight the range **A3:B8**, display the **Insert** tab and click **Column** in the **Charts** group. Select the **Clustered Column** option to create an embedded **Column Chart** as an object in the **Data** sheet.

4. The chart is active after creating it. Select to **Print**. Under **Settings**, **Print Selected Chart** is shown as the chosen option. Click the **Print** button to print just the chart.

> ℹ️ *Embedded charts are seldom printed by themselves as the quality is always of a poorer standard. Resizing does not help.*

5. Resize the chart to display all the column labels, horizontally. Print a copy of the chart and compare with the previous one.

6. Click away from the embedded chart on any cell and preview the worksheet to check that the chart and the data will fit on one page. Make any necessary adjustments.

7. To print a copy of the worksheet, display the **Print** options, **Print Active Sheets** is the default option. Click the **Print** button to print a copy of the whole worksheet including the chart.

8. Save the workbook as **Computer Data2**, the same file name.

9. Close the workbook.

Driving Lesson 95 - Revision

This Driving Lesson covers the features introduced in this section. Try not to refer to the preceding Driving Lessons while completing it.

1.   What tab is used to create a chart in *Excel*?

2.   Name the three most commonly used types of chart (the first three listed in the **Charts** group).

3.   Name the three other main chart types.

4.   If you were given the weekly sales figures for a company, what type of chart would you create to best demonstrate the data?

5.   What type of chart would you create to represent the breakdown of costs involved with producing a particular product?

6.   A **Bar Chart** and a **Column Chart** are similar, but what is the difference?

i   *Answers are shown in the **Answers** section at the end of this guide.*

If you experienced any difficulty completing this Revision refer back to the Driving Lessons in this section. Then redo the Revision.

Driving Lesson 96 - Revision

This Driving Lesson covers the features introduced in this section. Try not to refer to the preceding Driving Lessons while completing it.

1. Open the workbook **Analysis**.

2. Create a 2D pie chart on a new worksheet to be called **Sales Chart**, using the range **A3:B10**.

3. Add the chart title **Sales Analysis Figures**, show a **Legend** and apply **Data Labels** to show **Value** as **Outside End**.

4. Draw a text box over each segment and type in the appropriate name. Change the **Font** colour so the names can be easily read. Move each text box to a central position in the sector.

5. Format the title to be **16** point and **Blue** text.

6. Remove the **Legends** and print a copy of the pie chart.

7. The final chart should look as below.

Sales Analysis Figures

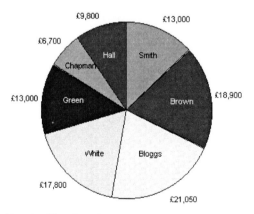

8. Close the workbook <u>without</u> saving.

If you experienced any difficulty completing this Revision refer back to the Driving Lessons in this section. Then redo the Revision.

Once you are confident with the features, complete the Record of Achievement Matrix referring to the section at the end of the guide.

Answers

Driving Lesson 10

Step 2   By a heavy border and the cell reference is displayed in the **Formula Bar**

Step 3   There are **3** by default - **Sheet1**, **Sheet2** and **Sheet3**

Step 4   a) **Increase Font Size**

         b) **Merge & Center**

         c) **Format Painter**

         d) **Fill Color**

Step 5   There are **5** groups displayed on the **Data** group

Step 6   The other group is called **Defined Names**

Step 7   **Exit**

Driving Lesson 11

Step 2   Click the **Close** button, located at the top right of the window or use the key press **<Alt F4>** or the **Excel** button at the top left and then **Close**.

Step 3   Three buttons; **Save**, **Undo** and **Redo**

Step 4   **<End>** →

Step 5   **1048576**

Step 6   **<Ctrl Home>**

Step 7   Press the Function key **F1**

Step 10 The **Home** button, ⌂.

Step 11 **Preview** is found under the **Printing** topic.

Driving Lesson 15

Step 7   The workbook **Budget** is active as it has just been opened.

Driving Lesson 30

Step 2   Column

Step 3   42

Step 4   21

Step 7   37

Driving Lesson 49

Step 4   £208

Step 7   £170

Step 9   £80

Answers

Driving Lesson 50

Step 4   **Friday** and 2008 was a leap year

Step 10 23725 days old at age 65 (approximately).

Driving Lesson 76

Step 6   £9876

Step 10 2008

Driving Lesson 77

Step 13 £388

Driving Lesson 83

Step 6   **=SUM(E6:E7)**

Driving Lesson 85

Step 1   **Relative Addressing**

Step 2   **$**

Step 3   a) **=C3+$E$5** b) **=D2+$E$5**

Step 4   **=E5+G6**

Step 5   When one cell contains information to be used by formulas in several locations.

Step 12 £763.62

Driving Lesson 95

Step 1   **Insert**

Step 2   **Column, Line** and **Pie**

Step 3   **Bar, Area** and **Scatter**.

Step 4   **Line** or **Column** chart

Step 5   **Pie** chart

Step 6   **Column** chart the data is represented by vertical columns and a **Bar** chart displays horizontal bars. The two axes change places.

Glossary

Addressing	A method of referencing cells, relative or absolute
Alignment	The position of data in a cell
AutoSum	A function to sum a range of numbers
Average	Function that adds a range and divides the number of numbers
Border	The edge of a cell, type and colour of line
Chart	A pictorial representation of data
Count	Function that displays the number of numbers in a range
Embedded Chart	A chart placed on a standard worksheet, usually with the source data
Excel	Spreadsheet software
Excel Options	Customisation of basic options
Fill Handle	A cursor used to copy data
Font	A type or style of text
Footer	Information appearing on the bottom of every printed page
Format	Changing the appearance of information
Formula	A calculation, can use values and/or cell references
Freeze Panes	Fixing information on screen so that it is not affected by scrolling
Function	Specialised formulas that make calculations easier
Header	Information appearing on the top of every printed page
HTML	A format that can be read over the Internet (HyperText Markup Language)
IF	Logical function that a carries out a test and performs one action if true and another if false
Maximum	Function that displays the largest number in a range
Minimum	Function that displays the smallest number in a range
Pixel	Small squares that make up the screen, normally 800 by 600
Range	A group of adjacent cells
Workbook	A spreadsheet file
Worksheet	A single page within a workbook
Zoom	Worksheet magnification on-screen only

Index

Record of Achievement Matrix

This Matrix is to be used to measure your progress while working through the guide. This is a learning reinforcement process, you judge when you are competent.

Tick boxes are provided for each feature. 1 is for no knowledge, 2 some knowledge and 3 is for competent. A section is only complete when column 3 is completed for all parts of the section.

For details on sitting ECDL Examinations in your country please contact the local ECDL Licensee or visit the European Computer Driving Licence Foundation Limited web site at http://www.ecdl.com.

Tick the Relevant Boxes **1**: No Knowledge **2**: Some Knowledge **3**: Competent

Section	No	Driving Lesson	1	2	3
1 Getting Started	1	Starting Excel			
	2	The Excel Screen			
	3	The Ribbon			
	4	Quick Access Toolbar			
	5	The Worksheet Window			
	6	Moving Around			
	7	Help			
	8	Preferences			
	9	Closing Excel			
2 Open and Close Workbooks	12	Opening a Workbook			
	13	Closing a Workbook			
	14	Using Scroll Bars			
	15	Opening Multiple Workbooks			
3 Creating & Saving Workbooks	17	Starting a New Workbook			
	18	Entering Labels			
	19	Entering Numbers			
	20	Saving a New Workbook			
	21	Saving a Named Workbook			
	22	Saving in Different Formats			
	23	Saving as a Template			
4 Formulas	26	Formulas			
	27	Brackets			
	28	AutoSum			
	29	Checking for Errors			
5 Workbooks	32	Multiple Worksheets			
	33	Switch Between Open Workbooks			
	34	Renaming Sheets			
	35	Copying and Moving Sheets			
	36	Inserting and Deleting Sheets			

Tick the Relevant Boxes **1**: No Knowledge **2**: Some Knowledge **3**: Competent

Section	No	Driving Lesson	1	2	3
6 Editing	38	Editing Cells			
	39	Delete Cell Contents			
	40	Using Undo and Redo			
	41	Ranges			
	42	Using the Fill Handle			
	43	Copying Cells			
	44	Moving Cells			
	45	Copying & Moving Between Workbooks			
	46	Finding Specific Text			
	47	Replacing Text			
	48	Sorting			
7 Printing	51	Printing			
	52	Print Preview			
	53	Page Setup			
	54	Margins			
	55	Printing a Selection			
	56	Headers and Footers			
	57	Print Titles			
	58	Displaying and Printing Formulas			
8 Formatting	61	Formatting			
	62	Bold, Italic & Underline			
	63	Font & Font Size			
	64	Format Number			
	65	Dates			
	66	Alignment			
	67	Changing Column Width			
	68	Changing Row Height			
	69	Inserting Rows and Columns			
	70	Deleting Rows and Columns			
	71	Adding Borders			
	72	Adding Colour			
	73	Rotating Text			
	74	Freezing Panes			
	75	Zoom			

Tick the Relevant Boxes **1**: No Knowledge **2**: Some Knowledge **3**: Competent

Section	No	Driving Lesson	1	2	3
9 Functions & Addressing	78	Functions			
	79	Count			
	80	Average and Round			
	81	Maximum and Minimum			
	82	IF			
	83	Relative Addressing			
	84	Absolute Addressing			
10 Charts	87	Introducing Charts			
	88	Creating Charts			
	89	Moving Charts			
	90	Chart Types			
	91	Copy, Move and Resize Charts			
	92	Formatting Charts			
	93	Chart Options			
	94	Printing Charts			

Other Products from CiA Training

CiA Training is a leading publishing company which has consistently delivered the highest quality products since 1985. Our experienced in-house publishing team has developed a wide range of flexible and easy to use self-teach resources for individual learners and corporate clients all over the world.

At the time of publication, we currently offer approved ECDL materials for:

- **ECDL Syllabus 5.0**

- **ECDL Syllabus 5.0 Revision Series**

- **ECDL Advanced Syllabus 2.0**

- **ECDL Advanced Syllabus 2.0 Revision Series**

Previous syllabus versions are also available upon request.

We hope you have enjoyed using this guide and would love to hear your opinions about our materials. To let us know how we're doing, and to get up to the minute information on our current range of products, please visit us at:

www.ciatraining.co.uk

Notes